GET WOKE
A YOUTH SUSTAINABILITY MANUAL

I AM A VESSEL

A CREATIVE EDUCATIONAL PLATFORM

This publication is the first publication of the I Am A Vessel creative educational platform titled, Get Woke™.

It provides an innovative perspective on the subject matter covered. It is sold with the understanding that the author and publisher are not engaged in professional counseling, teaching, or any other professional services. If assistance is required, the services of a competent professional should be sought.

©2020 by I Am A Vessel Youth Movement

Printed in the United States of America

ISBN: 978-1-7359105-0-5

Library of Congress Control Number: 2020920913

Published by I Am A Vessel®

P.O. Box 693 19012

Cheltenham, Pennsylvania

www.iamavessel.com

All rights reserved. This book and the information written is a compilation of material in connection with other copyrights and trademarks belonging to I Am A Vessel. The printing and publication of this text, or any part thereof, may not be reproduced in any manner whatsoever without permission from the publisher.

Dedicating this book to my amazing son, who is the catalyst and inspiration for me to never give up and to see the youth of this world thrive in every way imaginable beyond any limitation.

To my loving parents who rode this journey of revelation out with me to fulfill my calling.

Most importantly, to the Almighty up above.

Love you guys

CONTENTS

Preface ix
Introduction xv

1. FOUNDATION 1
2. EXPLORATION 14
3. WORTH 30
4. DIG DEEP 40
5. EYE SURGERY 56
6. LEVEL UP 70
7. NO LIMITS 86
8. LET THERE BE LIGHT 104
9. BRINGING IT ALL TOGETHER 111
10. VESSEL GLOSSARY 114

PREFACE

I'd like to begin by expressing how honored I am to create such a moment in time. What I'm about to present in this book will mark a new beginning for many youth, parents, and communities. Get Woke, which is the title of this book, is an introduction to the I Am A Vessel **Creative Educational Platform**. A timely resource developed as a result of my own intense journey of self-discovery. Within this book are words, thoughts, and information that will plant seeds of knowledge, vision, and wisdom for generations to come. Information that will be used to build young minds into solid structures with purpose and meaning.

My connection to the current concerns for youth and youth culture is quite dynamic. In relation to "getting woke," as like many who don't even recognize they have "fallen asleep," such was the case with myself. At a young age, I had built a life with a thriving career and business. I had lots of friends and thought I had everything all figured out.

I grew up in the city of Philadelphia in a two-parent home that provided me everything I needed. I attended public school and graduated from the Creative and Performing Arts High School in Philadelphia. Great memories were formed there. However, from as young as I can remember, I had two sides to my world. I was socially popular and yet, in many ways, rejected. Being exceptionally gifted creatively made me likable and fun to be around. Still, I had to endure many stigmas throughout my life.

My chocolate skin complexion was the butt of many jokes and the reason for many other unfavorable things. My uniqueness made me the oddball in my family and community. I was often purposely singled out on many occasions. My insight and brilliance got me put out of places I should have been nurtured to thrive in. I felt very undermined and emotionally displaced many times. When I tried to express my feelings, I risked sounding like "The Victim."

I grew up being rejected for the very things that made me...ME! I felt frustrated, and I learned from a very young age that the safest place to deal with my emotions was in my mind. I didn't realize that in doing so, I was digging a deep place of insecurity within myself. One not even of my own, but mainly as a result of the insecurities others felt towards me. This false sense of protection worked for about 25 years or so. However I began to realize my "strategy" had created barriers. I could reach a high level of achievement but my ability to go beyond seemed to have invisible limitations. I thought to work harder was the answer, and it wasn't.

I focused so much on success, that other areas of my life were left undone. After becoming a mother at the age of 30, things began to shift. A journey of true self-discovery had been assigned to my life. I say assigned because I was doing everything to grant success as I had always done, and yet it was clear that destiny had its way with me. A path that took everything in me to walk through, but boy, am I grateful I endured it. Had I not, I truly don't know where I would be. For the sake of not turning this book into an autobiography, let me fast forward a bit.

In 2014, I was at a crossroad in my career, which turned out to be the marking point that began a series of life-changing events. Things took a shift in gears, and a pathway towards my destiny was being made. I had no clue breaking beyond that invisible limitation, meant I had to remove the garbage I had allowed to hide within me over the years and heal through the side effects it caused.

Having spent the last 13 years building a successful career in the beauty and the arts industries, when I closed my thriving business, a beautiful salon in the swanky Spring Garden section in Philadelphia, I was being catapulted into the next phase of my life. The day when the central air unit of the million-dollar brownstone my salon operated in shut down (for the second time), it seemed to be the worst-case scenario. I did everything I could to find a solution that wouldn't cause me to invest thousands of dollars into a property I did not own. The devastating reality was that I had to re-locate.

Not only was I being considered as one of the best urban stylists and deemed the "Color Queen" in the city of Philadelphia, but I was also artistically thriving as a creative director as well. After closing my business, I began reflecting on the events that had occurred in my life thus far and decided to take some time from the hustle. I needed to focus on raising my son and figure out how the sudden changes I was experiencing were trying to lead me to re-direct my life. Boy, that was over six years ago, and my life certainly had been purposefully disrupted.

These last few years have been an intense process of dismantling everything I thought I knew about myself. A spiritual awakening Divinely timed to restructure my entire mental framework. A process that truly has built me from the inside out. Being a born entrepreneur, never having to clock in anywhere, extremely focused, and work-driven, my lifestyle certainly didn't reflect the capacity I have been designed to walk in. I realized my gifts of transforming the lives of people were being summoned to a higher level but that it first had to start within me!

I don't know where I would be without experiencing such a dramatic situation of losing almost everything I had worked so hard for. An experience where I had to dig deep down inside to learn myself and restart the process of building who I am, the right way this time! I began channeling my creative skills, artistic abilities, and resources to help women, children, and youth overcome their challenges in very unique ways. A gift of healing and creative problem solving I kept in the background of my career.

I started mentoring youth in Philadelphia and was on a gravitational road towards destiny. So here we are! As a result of searching to understand my true purpose, I decided to restructure my beauty business. I Am the proud CEO of Sina Marie Creative, I Am A Vessel Youth Movement 501C3, and I Am A Vessel Inc. Each of these is an umbrella in providing creative and transformative experiences, educational workshops and trainings, and preparing youth and community for the future.

The I Am a Vessel platform and Get Woke is about 3 ½ years in the making. Designed from the revelation I encountered mandating me to open the eyes of youth to deeper matters affecting their minds and spirits, much like I have overcome. As well as bringing awareness to the cultural, social, and economic influences affecting them. All to bring resolution to barriers in education, community, and communication. There's so much more to the story. Still, for now, I am excited to challenge youth culture not only intellectually but spiritually. I pray the knowledge released in this book will enter in every classroom, urban city, church, youth ministry, outreach program, and home as an instrument to act on this state of emergency regarding young generations.

INTRODUCTION

The actions of youth have been signaling for education and real-life to come together. It takes creativity to fuse education and life. Get Woke was created by the I Am A Vessel Youth Movement to help young adults gain a new sense of value for life, education, and to reshape youth culture. It is a journey for individuals seeking to strengthen the core of who they are. It focuses on the necessary purpose of self-knowledge and the importance for youth to cultivate themselves with intention in today's advanced world. Today's youth need tools to identify current struggles and self-limiting traits so they may be empowered on new levels.

The bigger picture is there is a need for deeper understanding prevalent for the sustainability of today's youth. Recent studies are showing the effects of the advancements in technology are having on humanity's ability to effectively communicate. It draws the world closer, and yet, there is a loss of deep and meaningful connection. As we stream, chat, and socialize via technology, we lose the inner need for togetherness, especially as generations move on.

Also, within the last decade, society has undergone major changes in many areas. Human connection and standards of living have been dramatically redefined.

For example, traditionally, the family structure was represented by man, woman, and their children. Today that structure has taken on many new normals. Even the imagery of the single mother has become familiar, not just in urban communities but within the culture. The ideals of marriage and family have diversified. They will most likely continue to do so, especially as many other standards change.

Watching the news certainly is different! The announcement of the news used to be a very serious job, and there seemed to be a no-nonsense policy. Today, the news has become much more entertaining. Depending upon which channel you may be watching, it's possible to mistake some news shows for reality tv!

Once upon a time, it would almost be impossible to get in touch with the President of the United States. In past times, writing a letter and hoping for a response was the best option for an average citizen wishing to contact him. Thanks to Twitter, your chances aren't as slim. Presidents are Tweeting and responding on social media just like everybody else! This changes society's expectations of government and authority.

Relationships have taken a toll in many ways as texting, dating, and hanging out all have different meanings. Youth today equate live chats, group streaming, and face timing with one on one contact. Family, news media, and government were all once a symbol of structure, and now today, the structure seems less important.

These are all just small examples of the many transitions happening in our reality. However, one must think about the changes in other areas such as transportation, occupation, communication, gender identification, and education. The question is, why aren't we exploring the effects of this change collectively on a larger scale?

Awareness of the shifts happening is necessary to be discussed with youth. Technology is amazing, but the advancement of humanity itself is a necessity in which healthy traditions and culture keep us connected. Educating youth on a deeper level should be a part of their formal training and development. I Am A Vessel is one of the first educational platforms focusing on this task more intricately.

The power of influence affects youths' minds, hearts, and spirits. As society advances, everyone, not just teens, must work harder to stay connected to hear their own inner disruption. With all the noise of the world, it's imperative to identify what's happening on the inside. Now more than ever, youth must learn how to strategize and strengthen themselves for physical and mental prosperity.

Get Woke is a self-education resource that combines youth empowerment and education together. We discuss important topics during this book from realistic, spiritual, and philosophical points of view, to present deep conversations uniquely. It is a crash course of complex topics in hopes of expanding the mindsets of youth. A fresh dose of reality to raise a higher consciousness to mobilize them and help them reshape their own culture.

Another key to the ascension of youth is helping them

understand the changes happening in and outside of them as they develop during a time when so much about our world is changing! Youth must recognize and nourish not only their cardinal selves but it's time for teens to be more responsible for their spiritual selves, which is the true essence of who they are!

Youth are being cultivated during times of major technological, social, political, and economic change; therefore, we must empower and prepare them for this modern era. Catch up to their quickly advancing minds and stabilize them. This book is a necessary awakening for youth and young adults. As we are in challenging times, sustainability is depending upon the substance and strength of the hearts, minds, and souls of youth and frankly everyone else as well. This is critical because spiritual maturity balances these earthly challenges.

It is the I Am A Vessel Youth Movement's hope that by empowering youth on a new level of self- awareness, we can help them all to Get Woke.

Get Woke is not only a book but a resource that combines youth empowerment and education together. It is what we are calling a **"Youth Sustainability Manual."** It is a tool for youth, families, and organizations to explore necessary information from realistic, spiritual, and philosophical points of view, to present deep conversations in a unique way amongst youth and young adults. The phrase Get Woke is a call to action for not only youth but adults, community, and society to act upon the current mandate screaming loudly.

We are in a time of "re": A time to replenish, redefine, rebuild, and reestablish youth, starting with youth culture.

We will be discussing the deeper meanings of life with youth culture, such as maturation, breaking barriers, spirituality, and sustenance in a more profound yet relatable way.

Where does the phrase **Get Woke** come from?

Get Woke is a spinoff of the term Stay Woke, which, according to Wikipedia, is an African American vernacular in English expression, which refers to continuing awareness of social issues. However, this book's objective is to help youth to Get Woke!

The term represents the objective of the I Am A Vessel Youth Movement to create a platform that educates youth on the unseen things affecting them because of societal changes, technology, social media, and losing human intimacy. Being woke means that one is aware and alert. To be alert is defined as being mentally perceptive and responsive, alive to what is going on. Perhaps we can conclude that not being alert on some level implies one is not living to their fullest potential. We live in such an action-packed society and being alert is a necessity for survival! Therefore, I Am A Vessel created this manual. An intentional resource providing the culture with the language, attitude, and mindset for survival in today's world but more importantly for life.

1
FOUNDATION

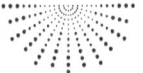

FOUNDATIONS ARE THE UNDERLYING PRINCIPLES. IT IS THE STRENGTH AND SUBSTANCE OF SOMETHING.

TAKE A MOMENT TO CONTEMPLATE YOUR FUTURE. WHAT DO you see? Somehow, we unconsciously see the future as a thing that miraculously appears. That's not the case. Our future is built layer by layer. We can make decisions that shape our individual circumstances. Imagine if you had to build your house by hand from the ground up. Think about all the hard work and the skill set needed to create a house that could meet your standards of safety, comfort, and style. Whether you realize it or not, you are building your future from the ground up. You **are** the foundation for your future.

Understand, you are **not** your body. Your physical body is the structure that holds who you are; it's your human shell.

However, your true self gives life to that shell. You are a spiritual being. Your thoughts, emotions, choices, and many other things translate to the world who you are **on the inside.**

We often define who we are or will become by our careers, but self-definition is more important than that. Who we are is how we communicate with the world and is an indicator of what we'll bring to the circle of life.

Life has proven that no matter what a person has been through, or **even** how successful a person becomes, one's inner foundation will be tested at a point in time—a test to see how well a person can navigate in times of adversity.

CONSIDER.

In 2008 the stock market crashed, devastating the world of wealthy investors. This crash was the largest point drop in history until 2018. Imagine if you were a billionaire investor. How would you have been able to handle such a loss? Some investors survived, and others didn't. Why? After losing millions, why did investors bounce back and others couldn't?

It's simple. When there is no money, friends, or resources, your belief system is your richest asset. How you **think** will determine your ability to survive **and** prosper.

Have you considered what your set of beliefs are?

REFLECT.

Take a moment to reflect on the famous people who have gained success, but something happened, and they turned to drugs, ruined their careers, and lost everything.

How about individuals who win millions in the lottery only to spend it all quickly, which forced them to go back to work, or worse, wound up in poverty.

In other words, things happen, and when they do, do we

give up? The difference between winning and losing when life's circumstances happen is the strength of your inner belief system. How you think determines **everything**!

By the time we are teenagers, our belief systems seem like they've already been shaped by our environments. Who we are and what we know seems final. Teens will find that as they mature, they must continually redefine and differentiate previous versions of themselves to continue to develop. This process includes staying connected with themselves by evaluating their mindsets.

Ah, staying connected during a time where social media and technology has much of the world's attention watching everyone else. Nevertheless, youth must focus and self-cultivate to become who they are.

Before going further let us give a full view of what we mean. Self-cultivation is not only an empowerment term. It is a mandate for every human being to intentionally **discover** who they are designed to be!

In other words, you are like a character in a painting-- discovering what the painting you exist in is all about *and* what the painter had in mind while creating the painting!

The secret of change is to focus all your energy not in fighting the old, but on building the new."

DAN MILLMAN, WAY OF PEACEFUL WARRIOR: A BOOK THAT CHANGES LIVES

BUILDING OURSELVES

Something amazing happens when we step up to the plate and build ourselves. A portal is shaped in the invisible world that houses the elements of progression, purpose, and destiny. An opportunity that only occurs with a decision to be more than we are today. Derived from a notion stirred up by a thought that says, "I'm more than what I currently see." One thought, one decision, and the actions of a made-up mind awaken the Divine power we each hold within us.

From the time we are born, inside of our little bodies, there is a glimpse of something great. We result from a dynamic process when a purpose and a spirit align and cross over from the spiritual world to the natural world. Whether youth realize it or not, everyone is born with a purpose inside of them. It's important to use the imagination to understand this because it allows us to grasp the full picture of who we are in humanity. We cannot count this off as religion or even a belief; this is a reality.

Unfortunately, youth are not pushed to acknowledge this part of themselves because it is a very real piece of who they are and the key to effectively developing into strong adults. Our emotions and personalities are spiritual. We cannot see them, and yet there's so much evidence of their existence in our lives. So, the mere responsibility set upon the youth to have self-control over their emotions and actions requires a level of understanding of things about who they are that they simply cannot see. Parts of themselves they came bearing here on earth **already** containing.

The I Am A Vessel slogan is "**Building youth from the inside out.**" Let's explore its meaning.

CONSIDER.

How do youth build themselves from the inside out? What does an architect use to build something? They need certain tools, but even with the right tools, how do they know where to begin?

The most efficient way to build anything is with a blueprint! Give yourself a pat on the back if you considered the importance of having a blueprint when building.

An artist or an architect uses a blueprint to ensure success. A blueprint allows the creator to align their effort with their vision. Vision is the creative process when the imagination is used to create something invisible into something tangible. Having a vision for the future means connecting to what has been established in eternity and seeing it in the present.

When one imagines themselves doing something amazing in a daydream, such as achieving a goal, being free from restrictions, or becoming the best version of themselves, they are connecting and recognizing the possibilities already inside of themselves! Youth may not realize it, but they have revelatory visions all the time about who they are and can be.

What then is the blueprint for one's life? We must ask this because we did not create ourselves. Do we look to our parents for our blueprint? Our teachers? Our friends? If youth want to reach their fullest potential, they must understand the blueprint to who they are is inside of them. This is what I Am A Vessel means when we say, "building from the inside out."

The tools given to humanity to build from the inside out is the mind, which is our operational system; along with our thoughts and words. These tools are used to activate our creative power! This is where the vernacular, a mind is a terrible thing to waste comes from.

It is also the reason a sound education and mindset are key for youth to properly develop. When the mind is used to its fullest potential, nothing is impossible. Building the minds of today's youth will require more than previous generations. As recent studies have been showing, there is a level of disconnect with current youth that is unlike any other generation. Many youths are facing inner challenges for many reasons. One evident thing, youth must be redeveloped for a new world on new levels! Youth should learn of the power within.

In doing so, they must be taught to understand their physical bodies are not who they are. It is only the structure, the human shell, which holds their true self. Youth must identify themselves as spiritual beings before anything else. Their spiritual selves represent their thoughts, emotions, choices, and many other things that translate to the world who they are…. on the inside.

LIVING YOUR BEST LIFE

I Am A Vessel defines living your best life as aligning yourself with who you are inside with your talents and gifts.

Self-cultivation starts by asking yourself if you're living your best life. Webster defines self-cultivation as developing one's mind through one's own effort. School gives youth education and develops their minds through the art of teaching. Self-cultivation is when youth hold themselves accountable for their **own** mental development. This process is where youth discover their true strength.

Why is self-cultivation the key to getting woke?

We each have an inner road map that is unique. It can't be accessed from the outside world; it can only be accessed from within.

Looking at the inside of who we are requires self-evaluation—our physical selves on the inside consist of organs, veins, and other important elements. But think about the spiritual aspects inside of us.

What's on the inside? How well do you communicate with yourself? What thoughts do you allow to roam through your mind?

When teens realize the quality of their lives is shaped by the quality of their thoughts, they can be empowered to consciously work on the inside.

How do we self-cultivate?

Self-cultivation is achieved by seeking to define ourselves. We achieve this by evaluating everything around us, exploring new things, creating standards, and developing necessary parameters. Yes, it takes all of that! We do this to eliminate aspects of ourselves that keep us from becoming the person we want to be. Youth could benefit from seeing themselves as individuals who change. The goal in life **is** growth!

So, growth starts with having a clear view of who you are. We are born as vessels because we contain inside of us special talents and gifts that contribute to all of humanity. Being a vessel is an identity. Saying the name, I Am A Vessel is a powerful acknowledgment of that identity.

Intentionally building ourselves builds our faith and belief we have been created for something special. How? Because acknowledging ourselves as Vessels reminds us that we each contain a value. The power of being a vessel is restorative. It counteracts negative self-identification because no matter our past, we are reminded of the future waiting for us to do something great.

Just think. When you say to yourself, "I am strong." It is a very powerful statement, but it is simply stating you have an attribute of strength. But when you say, "I Am A Vessel," you are defining who you were born to be, who you are now, and who you will be; and your value and worth! Powerful!

This is important because your name, what you call yourself, and what you think about yourself has the power to shape who you are. Since maturation is much about shaping young adults for their future, identity is the starting point for youth to build their inner foundations. Many youths who feel lost and uncertain about themselves often do, because they have not taken the time to define themselves. Our name, I Am A Vessel is a tool for individuals of all ages to begin that process.

THE VESSEL

> **A vessel is a large ship or container that carries goods from one place to another. We, too, carry special gifts inside of us for a great purpose.**

A VESSEL SHIP or container is special because of its purpose. They each carry valuable items from one point to another. Vessels are often attributed to being a transporter of something sacred. For instance, a vessel transporting food would be a transporter of the necessities sustaining a region of people. Here's the correlation:

A **human vessel** is a biblical term acknowledging how humanity is intentionally created. When we look at a person, what we really should see is the capabilities in them to solve a problem or change the world! You **are** a vessel. Everything you are born to be is inside of you from the very beginning of your conception in your potential. Potential is not guaranteed to turn into greatness. It stays inside dormant, waiting to be activated through your efforts. Activating yourself as a vessel happens when you choose to put your gifts into action. You must use your positive beliefs and natural abilities to tap into the best version of yourself.

Youth should understand their inner gift is **not** their identity but their abilities. When youth learn to clearly define their identities, they can more effectively demonstrate their abilities. Which is why they should be intentional with their development.

CONSIDER.
If you were a ship, what would you contain?

DEFINING WHO YOU ARE

In 1993 legendary artist Prince announced he was changing his name. He would no longer go by Prince but would be identified by a symbol instead. This move created problems for his career as his fans were not receptive to the idea of their favorite artist having no name. They called him the artist formerly known as Prince. In the 1970s, when Prince signed with Warner Brothers, he signed over the rights to his name, allowing the record company to own his trademark, which gave them legal control over his brand.

According to Prince, this affected his ability to freely create music. But in 1993, Prince devised a plan that would indirectly regain ownership of his brand. He renamed himself and created new music under the symbol, which allowed him the ability to define himself and his sound as he wished. Once his initial contract was over, Prince then brilliantly resumed creating music under his original name.

Here's the deal. In this world, we either define who we are or allow someone else to do it for us.

So how exactly do we define ourselves? Again, our **belief systems**. Though we define ourselves by setting standards, a set of beliefs we live by that create boundaries to help navigate us in life. Boundaries are imperative to keep us safe. Our spirituality is important because what we believe should be in harmony with the laws of life itself.

While everyone may have their own ideals, we learn through forms of established laws of creation such as nature, physics, community, and many other things. We learn from them because of the boundaries revealed by the physical and invisible limitations and expectations that they determine.

In that same manner, youth must be guided to establish standards, and as they mature, they will most likely have the tools to effectively shape them more specifically for themselves.

SETTING STANDARDS

We should not just set standards only because of our opinions or experiences. Again, our foundations that are often tested should be rooted and established in truth.

Although---- we may have the capacity to build **from** a foundation, it is the **existing** foundation that gives us the ability to create in the first place. Just like an architect, it is fundamental to have knowledge of what that foundation entails before we began the process of building and creating anything! Same things we need to consider when building ourselves and defining who we are.

When we consider foundations and standards, whether in the physical or spiritual aspect, we recognize that there are parts of our own foundations we must discover to effectively define ourselves and create a belief system that's built to last.

The starting point for setting standards is God. Our lives should reflect God's love for us and serve as a precursor for how we love ourselves and others. Love connects, heals, restores, builds and many other things. Let's take a second to look farther. Here's something to consider:

We hear so many stories of self-discovery and how it's a journey through love. Part of that discovery is learning that love cannot be just draw from anywhere! Although many may try to. However, love is an innate connection that has two things that confirms it…. spirit and truth. Not even words and what someone says can prove that love is real. Something on the inside of each of us innately identifies with real love.

Even in the Bible, when asked what is the most important commandment, Jesus said: Love the Lord your God with all your heart, soul and mind. And secondly, love thy neighbor as yourself. (Matt. 22:36-39)

Here's the deal, it's about substance. Whatever is the substance of who you are establishes your foundation. Or rather, whatever is the substance of your foundation shapes who you are. Current youth culture is being developed during critical times of change. It's imperative that we evaluate the substance and stability of their foundations as a whole. Let's begin this process.

2
EXPLORATION

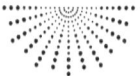

THE PREREQUISITE FOR YOUTH TO GET WOKE IS A JOURNEY through the unfolding of how they think. The youth must look outside themselves, so to speak, and have a panoramic view of what their culture looks like today to better understand their personal cultures.

More specifically, there is a need for youth to explore and examine their collective inner worlds and cultural sphere. Inner world meaning, how they feel, think, and respond. Cultural sphere, meaning the habits, ideals, and rituals as a generation they are developing in.

> Exploration is the activity of searching and learning about something. It is the discovery of resources and information. For youth to balance their mind frames with the rapid changes in culture, they must transition to a new level of maturity. Maturity is set in motion

when one examines the nature of certain behaviors.

Let's do some examination.

WHO ARE YOU?

While speaking at one of the inner-city high schools in Philadelphia, founder Sina Marie Washington spoke with thirty sophomore, junior, and senior high school students. These students were studying to be fashion designers. Sina Marie was a guest speaker sharing her experience and knowledge in the beauty and fashion industries. After presenting to the students some of her dramatic designs, she further engaged them in a trivia game surrounding the subject.

To Sina Marie's surprise, the students could not answer the questions. One student yelled out, "We don't know any of these answers!" They all laughed. Finally, curious to understand more about the students, Sina Marie asked, "Who wants to be a fashion designer of the future?" Except for one student, no one raised their hand. She became confused.

How could it be that a class full of design students had no desire to become the very thing they were studying to be? Fashion is fun! Isn't it? She then directed the students to clear their desks and had a serious conversation with them.

Her next question was, "Who are you?" The class ignited, and students expressed their concerns about not truly knowing. One student responded to the question by stating that she was a "project kid." Project kid, meaning she lived in low-income housing. Sina Marie had to correct the student by informing her that: where she lives does not define who she is. That's when Sina realized she was there for a bigger purpose than to discuss fashion.

One student boldly asked her, "How did you know who you wanted to be and what you wanted to do in your life?" She answered the students simply, "**By exploring**."

The challenge for today's youth is that the tools the creator has blessed them with are not being used correctly. Youth today are becoming conditioned to using their eyes to explore! We were blessed with two feet for a reason! Our feet can never teach us how to see, and our eyes alone cannot physically take us to new places.

Exploring via the internet is a modern form of exploration, but it is limited. Youth should consider the benefits of real exploration. The people they will meet; the things they will see along the way; the energy they will feel; awakens something on the inside of them. Discovering who they are is a journey that must be encountered by physically exploring new things.

Humanity's greatest resource will always be the earth and the fullness therein. Society must continue to push youth to explore less via the internet and more in real-time. The mind needs to process naturally as opposed to being locked into escapades of virtual experiences.

In fact, the Merriam-Webster dictionary defines experience as **direct observation** of or participation in events as a basis of knowledge. Another definition is practical knowledge, skill, or practice derived from direct observation or participation in events or in an activity.

. . .

CONSIDER.

When youth learn and explore via the internet, should they truly consider it as an experience? A person who attends college via the internet, can they say they know what like to be a college student? Something amazing happens when youth put down their smartphones and live in the moment. They gain capacity for who they are destined to be!

EXPANSION

Expansion is a thing formed by the enlargement, broadening, or development of something.

MANY ACCOMPLISHED people talk about their love of traveling, and they often credit a portion of their success to their explorations. The connection between expansion and exploring is significant in our lives, and youth should clearly understand how.

Exploring ourselves and the world expands our ability to receive new knowledge. It is said that the more a person knows, the further they'll go in life. Have you ever been introduced to something new, and you really couldn't get into it? You didn't even try because you had your mind already made up.

For example, let's say, one of your friends took a trip to Africa over the summer, and he came back listening to African hip-hop. He came to your house, excited to share his new discovery. You listened to it and said to yourself, "I'm not feeling it." You just can't understand the big deal. However, after listening to the music while chilling, you google the artist. Because of researching the artist and listening to the music repeatedly, you appreciate African hip hop. Suddenly, you have a *new* favorite artist, and *you* now "put people on" to a new sound. Your friend is looking at you like... really?

Think about it. If you wanted to learn a technique in basketball or applying makeup, you would most likely check out a YouTube tutorial. Whether you know it or not, YouTube is wildly popular because it's a form of exploration that combines research and exposure. Youth must use a similar approach to successfully research their inner selves to broaden their perspectives and develop on another level.

THE CULTURE

Culture is manifestations of art and human intellectual achievement regarded collectively. It is accomplished through a spiritual connection with one another.

YOUTH CAN'T EXPLORE themselves without exploring the culture. **Why?** Because culture is probably the #1 influence in their lives today. Youth should ask themselves the following question: Is culture new age education?

Culture shapes so much of them! Their opinions, thoughts, habits, interests, language, and music they listen to reflects culture.

How? Culture is the hub in which generations operate. Describing culture is difficult. It's invisible and yet very present. Culture is a way of a group of people, an integrated pattern of knowledge, beliefs, and behaviors. On a deeper level, it is the attitudes, values, morals, goals, and customs shared by society.

How is culture created, **and what are the influencing factors?**

Quora, a question and answer website, says culture is **learned** rather than innate and is repeatedly **passed on** from one generation to another. It allows **continuity** of a body of knowledge and beliefs. So, culture is learned and passed on. Powerful for something that begins invisibly.

If so, youth may want to ask themselves, "What are the current cultures of today, and what realities have they shaped for their generation?" Let's explore more about this now.

CULTURE CREATES REALITY

Fifteen years ago, cell phones were not a part of everyday life. Back then, if you asked to use someone's phone, the response would differ greatly from today. You would be directed to a location in someone's home where you could find the phone base.

For those of you too young to remember, wireless telephones were very popular. It came in two parts: the base where the phone rested or charged, and the phone itself. If the phone went missing, it featured a button used for signaling its location. The phone could turn up anywhere: between the couch cushions, under the bed, or in your back pocket!

Today, wireless phones are becoming a thing from the past. Cellular phones made their debut in 1973 and became available to the public in 1984. Since then, the newer and more improved smartphone is the choice of communication. According to the most recent report by the U.S Center for Disease Control National Health Information Survey, 42.8% of American households still use a wireless phone as of December 2017.

Current numbers have changed, and the percentage is probably even less than that. Smartphones are taking over because it's all about functionality. They have become such a commodity that the price consumers are willing to pay has skyrocketed from a few hundred to eight hundred dollars or more. Because of the expensive price tag, financing smartphones have become a way of life.

WOW! Who would have ever thought the day would come when smartphones needed to be leased, like a car! Leasing a car seems reasonable, but a **phone**? The catch is this, by the time the lease of the phone is paid, there is a newer and more advanced version available. This illustrates how culture is used for financial gains by companies and should be an example for youth to understand their need for a cultural reality check.

<u>Consider.</u>
What led to leasing smartphones?
How did society become so co-dependent on them?
The answer is **influence**!

Culture subconsciously influences people to adopt habits and rituals. However, culture can unify people and build communities in amazing ways.

As young adults, it's important to know how the influence of culture can have a negative effect. Youth are valuable in culture and need to know how marketing, technology, and social media strategically influence their choices for profitable gain. A lot of marketing strategies are based on the predictability of teen behavior, in which we will further examine.

Advertisers understand the power of influence and project celebrities, lifestyles, and trends as being cool even when it's not in teens' best interests. It's a cultural trend that has increased youth vulnerability. The manipulation of these influences can  cause youth to become materialistic, overly competitive, and disconnected, which then leads to other inner struggles.

While we recognize the necessity of advancement in technology, we also must acknowledge the responsibility it imposes on each of us. Society must consciously work to stay grounded and in touch with real life, especially as artificial intelligence and virtual reality becomes advanced and are integrated into our paradigm.

The world is expanding right before our eyes. We must consider the effects to youth and their mental capacities; as a result, to so much access to information.

The senses are windows or portals into the inner parts of who we are.

SINA MARIE

A CULTURAL SENSE OF REALITY

A sense is a physiological capacity of organisms that provides data for perception.

Here is the main reason youth need the wisdom of adults. Because adults have lived long enough to understand cause and effect. Which is why they consider things that many youths may not. The things that become important down the line, adults can see a mile away. The culture of youth could use some sifting.

The purpose of exploring culture is not to impose fear but wisdom. Wisdom is protection over one's life. Protection is one of the many topics that concerned parents and adults are always thinking about when it comes to youth and young adults. If today's youth understood that their minds are like gardens, they could protect themselves from unnecessary "trauma."

Every generation faces a "threat," so to speak. In the '50s and '60s, many youths had to face racism and segregation; in the '80s, the crack epidemic threatened culture, which brought about the infamous "Say No to Drugs" campaign. These are just a few examples. Although many things are happening within culture today, a major concern is the protection of youth and their minds. So much about how society communicates is perception-based, and there seems to be a need for more reality to balance it all.

Youth should know their senses are directly connected to how they perceive everything in life. Perception is based on how we receive information through our senses. This means that your eyes, ears, mouth, and hands are more important than you may realize. Yes, one is taught that through the senses, we hear, see, smell, taste, and feel, but they are responsible for much more than that.

> **The senses are windows or portals into the inner parts of who we are.**

Youth should know their inner selves, which includes the heart, mind, and soul, which are directly influenced by them. So, the senses play a major role in thoughts, moods, and feelings. The things that make up the real you, therefore, youth must learn the importance of being selective in what they allow to have access to their senses. Picture a city with no walls, gates, or borders. This is what it's like to live without structure, limitations, or standards. The level of vulnerability it impedes on young minds is disturbing. Protecting the sensors is necessary for the mental and physical well-being of youths.

For the sake of being clear, here are traditional examples of how the senses are used to influence the mind. For instance, a party can seem so much fun while the lights are off, and the music is going, but the minute the lights are turned on, the mood or perception of the moment shifts.

Another example is, during a scary movie, when certain music plays it triggers the mind via sound in a way that causes fear. Technology, reality tv, social media, likes, follows, video games, photographic filters, and even music lyrics are being more influential through the senses than ever before. In current culture, happiness, beauty, success, experiences, and even fame seems based on perception versus fact.

The bottom line is there seeming to be a shortage of reality. It can be exhausting thinking about all the cultural factors society has become accustomed to that may be considered unhealthy. What youth listen to, look at, and speak about impacts their personal lives, and youth should have a practical sense of awareness!

CULTURAL IDENTITY

According to the World Economic Forum, we have entered a new era of economics, fashion, textiles, and especially technology. In the next 20 to 30 years, Artificial Intelligence (AI), which we see the beginning of its integration in society, is expected to replace many current jobs. Major changes in economics mean more opportunities and new job markets.

<u>Consider.</u>
What else does this mean for youth culture?

It means more outside influence. Social Media is advancing quickly, and other platforms are becoming more advanced. Human interaction is at close viewpoints. People are creating their own multi-functional communities. Closer access emphasizes greater levels of influence. Because of this, youth have been known to abandon their individuality to adopt the personal habits, style, interests, and even career paths of their favorite "Social Media Influencers." Why is this? Because identity **is** culture! Inspiration is great.

However, youth should guard themselves against the obsession with popularity as it may cause them to change who they naturally are to look popular. There's nothing wrong with being popular, but if you must become a different person, then the cause is not worth it!

Here's something to think about. Pre-social media, there were a lot more types of people. It was easy to identify where a person resided just by looking at them. If one traveled from Philadelphia to visit relatives in Georgia, there would be a distinction in the way people dressed and styled their hair, especially young women.

Trends hit up north a few years before they would become a "thing" in the south. Partially because Southerners have different core interests than Northerners. However, since the rise of social media, that is no longer the case. Southern girls are wearing the same color hair, frontal wigs, and dramatic eyelashes as the average Northern girl of today.

While this is not a negative change, the question is: Is society becoming single-minded? Sounds dramatic, but the obsession with likes and followers could develop such a crazy reality. Think about it. If social media influences identity **and** culture, how deeply are teens being influenced? The internet is a great way to explore, but it should not be the foundation for anybody to discover who they are.

BUILDING NEW YOUTH CULTURE

Why is building a new youth culture so important in today's world? Opportunity is happening! This is one of the main reasons for our collaboration of exploring during this book.

Technology is making the world condensed. A smaller world surprisingly means more access, but it also means more competition **and** places a higher level of responsibility on humanity. Problems are being solved **and** created simultaneously. Because of this, knowing who you are is pertinent to your prospering.

As mentioned, the youth cannot afford to be dormant. Urban youth culture is in demand, but there are many things youth are not aware of. The culture must continuously prepare its members on a larger scale, not only because of the changes but also for dibs on all the opportunities. Institutions are testing and investing in the preparation of new business models and markets, and that means they need young minds. You are the **Vessels of the Future**!

The amazing part is that youth today are extremely intelligent, resourceful, and have quick minds. Youth are strong and resilient, so nothing is impossible for them!

A MINDSET TO WIN

As youth mature, they will learn that self-discipline is the remedy to a lot of things and is key to leading healthy inner lives. The advice to youth, with regards to the influence of culture is, "Be yeasty and not spongy." Sponges absorb everything wet it encounters and is easily weighed down. They harbor lots of bacteria because of it's porous nature.

On the other hand, yeast is a catalyst, therefore, it influences. It multiplies within itself and causes flour to rise. Youth should be self-sufficient and real influencers for the culture. Real influencers bring the uniqueness of the mind to diversify the norm. They have a strong sense of self and impact the lives of others to be more authentic. Young generations should not allow a culture to control them. Put culture in its place! This is what it means to be a Vessel!

3
WORTH

Let's explore the productivity of youth culture, which we will do in an unfolding manner. Some topics we are exploring may not personally apply to every youth or young adult but does as a culture. As they are trending topics and areas, every youth should be made aware of, such as time and value, which is directly connected to self-worth.

Time and value, where should we start? They are important factors youth need clarity on because the current culture's value system focuses on appearances. This trend is a disadvantage to youth because they are growing up in an era that underestimates the value of process! Speed and quantity are celebrated over the process and quality of things! This gives youth a skewed understanding of how life works.

As a result, many often lack the patience of endurance, which is learned from working hard and developing stamina. Instead, goals and careers are inspired by easy money and fame. Mentors are social media influencers, and many people, not just youth, look for success in templates. This "copycat" behavior can be partially responsible for the urgent need for youth to self-develop more quickly.

THE VALUE OF TIME

Time is considered one of life's most valuable assets because it's one of the few things we can never get back.

FOR YOUTH TO become the best versions of themselves, they need the aptitude for patience and process. They must be wise enough to realize, although culture demonstrates that speed is more important, nothing is more guaranteed than investing time in their development.

There are certain systems of learning key to human intellect. The connection between time and value will forever relate to mental development and the process of maturity.

One of the characteristics of a mature teenager is they understand how to delegate their time to do things. If you want to know what you value, look at where most of your focus is. It is a proven theory that people generally **lack** focus for things they don't value. Time is one of the most valuable things in life. It is said to be more valuable than money.

How? Time is the space in which we **make** money. That's the meaning behind an hourly pay rate. People who earn more in salary are considered to hold *more value* because they either spent *more time* educating themselves or put *more time* in at a job. That nothing can be accomplished without it proves that time is more valuable than money.

Culture has programmed our thinking to believe that convenience and speed mean better, and sometimes it does! We benefit from companies such as Uber, Uber Eats, Cash App, and Amazon, who use this philosophy. We benefit, but there are underlying factors. The more society support concepts that promote speed as being better, in some ways, we create a paradigm that speeds up our own human experience.

Speed causes humanity to function off adrenaline versus a natural rhythm and pace in sync with life and nature. Culturally, society must consciously balance speed and convenience with patience and a healthy perspective of value. Peace should always remain more valuable than having everything at our fingertips. Period.

CONSIDER.

There was a time when how long a person lived granted them respect. Is this still true? Does a person's age grant them respect? Is age still valued, or have everyone become equal?

FROM THE BEGINNING

Young adults sometimes have this unspoken belief that their youth will last forever. Partially because there is so much open space to do whatever they want to do, or at least it seems like it. Perhaps the way culture views time is limited.

How do we grasp a true value for something we often take for granted?

Maybe because society teaches that time is numbers on a clock. Humanities limited perspective views time as the 24 hours within the day or 60 minutes within an hour. For some, it is as valuable as the time they spend on the treadmill, taking a nap, or waiting for dinner to be ready. Oh, but time is much more valuable than that. It is a precious gift that allows all of humanity to live and participate in a personal and collective process created for a purpose. A purpose decided before we were born.

How is time defined? Time is the indefinite continued process of existence and events in the past, present, and future regarded as a whole.

Let's break this down.

Time is a process; existence; continual; events; past; present; and future all at the same time. Woah! That's deep. That's major! Perhaps time deserves more respect than it receives? Because it is continual, it always has and will always exist. Therefore, it must hold the secrets of life.

No matter the age, there is a timely expectation for moments in life. By the age of 1, one is expected to walk, begin talking, and feeding oneself. By the age of 5, one is expected to clearly communicate verbally and tie one's shoe. Around the age of twelve, one is expected to be responsible for one's actions on a profound level, and puberty is expected to have taken action.

Whether youth wants to acknowledge this fact or not, there is a timely expectation over one's life right now! A mandate of maturity and a responsibility to make right choices and decisions. The teen and young adult years are critical training ground for life. Youth today must adhere to the inner voice inside of them, that is there to align them to the timely expectations over their youthful years and navigate them towards their destinies.

That's right! Many youths believe that they are not responsible for governing themselves and their decisions because they are young. As we learn from nature, life is a process. From the day one is born, time ticks and expectations are set into action. It is a blessing because it simply means you are alive!

It is I Am A Vessel's hope to inspire youth beyond the average come what may come what goes mindset. Youth should wake up every morning with an empowering thought that helps them to make the most of their time.

A thought such as: May I grow in wisdom and conduct myself accordingly with the timely expectations over my life. This simply teaches youth to acknowledge the Vessels they are and the mandate over all of humanity, no matter the age, to actively forge towards destiny!

TIME REVEALED

Hidden in all of creation, which is everything that exists, are clues about time. Time is revealed in nature, the universe, and human creation.

ONE OF THE unfortunate things about current culture is the avoidance of educating youth on the spiritual things of life. As it is detrimental to their development, logical understanding, and mental health. When youth are empowered with deeper knowledge, they are given the capacity to receive revelation. A revelation that enlightens them on the expectations that their family, schools, relationships, and life itself may have of them.

The universe, which makes up the stars, moon, everything up in the sky and beyond, teaches a great lesson. While there is so much to know about it, what we do know is that the sunsets and rises at certain times; the moon and the stars light the sky at night; the planets circle the earth in Divinely order changing seasons; and everything working together sets time into motion. This teaches us a great lesson! It teaches humanity that time constructs order. There is an order in which everything must operate promptly.

Once a baby is conceived inside of a mother's womb, there are 9 months for him or her to fully develop. During these 9 months, a baby that starts as an embryo goes through phases and stages of growth. When it is time to be born, the mother's body naturally goes through physical changes to prepare for the baby to be birthed. When it is time, no matter if the baby or the mother is ready or not, the birth will need to take place. We learn from human creation that time is a catalyst for growth, and the evidence is change. The wisdom of nature and creation will always lead us to the truth. It has been designed that way.

Agriculture is the study of cultivating the land. It is a historical source of wealth and power and is a sustainer of people and animals. It represents growth and intentionality.

What clues do nature and agriculture give us about time? This could get extremely in-depth in which that is not the purpose of this topic. However, it is intended for youth to gain a deeper level of respect for their lives in which it is greatly connected to how they spend their time.

Agriculture is one of the first forms of business and trading. Provision for families and entire communities depended greatly on the success of not just one day, but an entire season. Farmers and sharecroppers had to master and plan the timing of each day, month, and season to ensure they could be able to survive during off-seasons. Watering their crops at certain times of the day maintained their land. By the end of the season, they would be harvesting what they needed to feed their families or maintain their businesses.

Without the gift of time, survival couldn't have been secured, much like our own lives. If youth want to "secure the bag" on any level, they must set good habits with their time. How they govern their daily lives eventually shapes their entire month, year, and future. One moment lays the foundation for the other. Remember, time is continuous, and so is planting and harvesting. There is no pretending when it comes to planting.

Eventually, whatever time and effort one invests will show by the crop harvested. Youth should view time as a seed. It is an investment to secure their futures. No one is ever too young to do that! The beautiful thing about time is that it is renewed each day. Every day we get another to be our best selves. That's the blessing of being human.

REFLECT.
What seeds are you planting with your time? How can you use your time more wisely?

THE VALUE OF EDUCATION

Many teens question the value of going to school and getting an education. Especially when they see the endless possibilities that technology and social media **appear** to offer. Many people are creating futures in untraditional careers that seem to require minimal knowledge. Teens should know that value in education extends beyond the obvious. Education is an inheritance. It is **not free!**

However, youth who attend public schooling can receive an education at absolutely no cost to them. The fact that 12 years of education is available for free is obvious proof that the gains are BIG! There are fundamental, technical, and social skills we learn that are necessary for a good quality of life, which happens during our 12 years of schooling. We undergo major social preparation needed to operate in the real world. The training towards adulthood and life during the high school years is invaluable as it cultivates who we are.

This greatly extends beyond the classroom because youth learn through their relationships, exposure, and experiences. What often prohibits students from benefiting is their own resistance to learning, building relationships, and following instructions.

Education is also a symbol of freedom. If teens considered how many youths, just like them, across the globe, fought for quality education, they would appreciate theirs much more.

Students spend countless hours attending school every

day and probably never stopped to think about just how much time and energy they invest there. It's worth taking a moment to stop and ask themselves, are they doing their part in making the most of it?

Wealth is obtainable by the measure that one will use their mind. Because education is **how** the mind is developed, it's safe to say it should not be taking too lightly.

So, what is the ROI of education?

ROI is a business term acronym that refers to the return on investment. It is the profit made by a product.

TIME/ VALUE RATIO

During the I Am A Vessel co-ed program, many students reflected on their time management. They admitted that they hadn't thought about it. We took the time to focus a great deal on visually showing students what the daily distribution of their time looks like because the opportunities of the youthful years are so important. Certain windows of opportunity for many people happen in their youth.

Windows that are literally portals to their future. Time prepares youth and their minds for the next level. Youth must shift the ideology of their time from minutes on a clock and see time as preparation and opportunity.

Youth spend 8 hours in school every day, which leaves them with 16 hours to accomplish everything they need to do within the rest of their day, including sleep. The question is, how well are they managing the remainder 16 hours each day?

This is the necessary inner reflection needed for youth to move beyond certain "habitual constraints" they may have because of cultural habitation and constructs that can often stagnate their progress.

What are we saying? Some of the bad habits that many youths have may be because of wasting their time on the wrong things. Stemming from an incorrect outlook on how precious time is. Partially because culturally, time and value has been redefined, displaced, and prioritized in things that are non-essential.

Ask yourself, is time an important factor in your life or do you just do what you want when you want with little to no consequence?

4
DIG DEEP

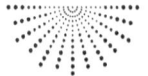

As communication becomes more innovative, the world appears to expand within itself. Still, really everything is more condensed, as mentioned previously. It can feel overwhelming because expansion creates more space. More space means more information, exposure, options, and influences.

Youth are not technically prepared to handle this new space and haven't been given many tools to safely navigate. First and foremost, they must get conscious about the new level of responsibility to not only develop standards but to create **mind protectors**.

Some challenges we see effecting youth culture results from the idol and slothful like attitudes and behaviors culturally acceptable. Some clothing brands, music artists, and social media influencers subliminally promote this behavior. What's interesting is that there seem to be two extremities. On the one hand, many youths are unfocused, and yet their brilliance is undeniable!

The culture needs to build a vision for themselves that surpasses this gray area, rise beyond entertaining such behaviors. Young men and women need to demonstrate inner power to exceed beyond their environments, circumstances, and intrinsic cultural behaviors.

We protect our physical selves all the time. On an extremely cold day when the wind chill is fierce, and the temperature is minus zero degrees, would it be recommended for someone to walk outside without a coat, hat, or gloves? The weather doesn't necessarily require that one must stay inside. However, certain precautions to protect oneself from the cold, illnesses, frostbite, and other things are necessary. The same level of protection is needed for general mental and spiritual health.

BEYOND THE SURFACE

Board games, coloring books, puzzles, Uno cards, crossword puzzles, match, Connect the Dots, mazes, newspaper comics, Rubik's Cube, Hangman, Twister, Hopscotch, and Tic-Tac-Toe were once popular interactive activities used to build the minds of youth. Because the mind is a muscle, certain activities strengthen its ability to problem solve and comprehend.

These activities aren't as popular today as culture doesn't focus as much on traditional ways of mentally exercising. The benefit of having to think through something to achieve a goal is pricelist. Trying to figure out if to go left, right, up, or down with a Rubik's Cube builds a deeper understanding that our minds, eyes, and actions all work together to determine certain outcomes.

There is something that's lost when manual activities are traded in for electronic or digital activities. Youth are being taught application without comprehension visually equivalent to a robot. Add that movement is being lost, and youth obesity is on the rise.

Perhaps, if we look beyond the surface, we should question the possibilities that youth could be lacking key components in their development, which affects their ability to consciously make productive decisions.

How many youths today are being raised with daily, weekly, and monthly rituals that teach them the art of maintaining a particular lifestyle? Traditional household rituals that were once a lifestyle seems less important in culture. Rituals such as setting the dinner table, spring cleaning, and seasonal packing all played a role in maintaining order and structure in our environments.

As it is in the natural, so is it in the spiritual. Our physical environment will reflect or affect our inner world. An exchange takes place when we effectively make choices that keep things in order. Order eliminates dysfunction, which results in something amazing called progress. Perhaps, to make up for areas in which culture has fallen short in preparing today's youth, we should teach them to intentionally go deeper and look beyond the surface.

Not only the surface of the world around them but more important, inside themselves. Reading this text is a journey looking at youth culture but only as a pathway to rethink what it all means. By the end, the goal is to strip down the culture to refill youth with the Divine knowledge that will empower their futures. Which is why we will consistently address the mindsets of the youth.

Why? Because contrary to what culture promotes, the minds of the youth are the technology of the future! The mind is the leading operating system over all things. Youth will need to adopt a new level of respect for the value of their minds, how to use it, protect it, heal and elevate it for the development and sustainability of humanity in this new era.

STIMULATION

Stimulation is the encouragement of something to make it develop or become more active, arousing interest, enthusiasm, or excitement.

As YOUNG ADULTS, youth are responsible to actively participate in their own mental progress. The future is literally depending on two things from youth culture, mental innovation, and spiritual maturation. **Mental innovation** requires the ability of youth to align their perception, intelligence, and intuition together so they may function more effectively.

A sharpness that cultivates a realm for youth to have dominion over their thinking and living in society. This innovation also serves as a realm of protection from the overload of technology and societal instability that may result as the world advances.

It's significant for youth culture to understand how overstimulation affects their focus. Overstimulation can become seriously distractive. Youth may not realize how their minds are being stimulated while surfing the internet or social media. Constant images and information arousing them in ways that may be considered inappropriate.

There used to be a time where youth would be protected from certain images, conversations, and information until they reached a certain level of maturity. That is no longer the case and so mimicking adult-like behaviors and attitudes has become the norm.

For instance, the pictures that promote certain behaviors as acceptable, a growing trend we see on social media: teens posting pictures of themselves with their middle fingers up promoting an I don't care attitude; or even pictures of young women posted in their underclothes promoting themselves as young vixens. Youth must dig deeper into today's superficial culture and exercise mental strength and good judgement.

There are many behaviors and influences that aren't necessarily harmful, but that influences teens' identities in non-productive ways. But when youth know themselves on deeper levels, they are not easily influenced. They create healthy boundaries to protect themselves from being affected by the exposure available to them.

Youth can only operate effectively in the culture at the level of their maturity. Today's youth must "**Debo**" over many influences affecting them. There is a mental fight to keep their minds healthy and positive! They must understand what they see, hear, and read will influence how they perceive everything dimensionally within themselves, their families, and communities. It's all relative; As the Vessel, symbol demonstrates you are a community within yourself!

The biggest threat to young generations is living below the standard of who they were created to be. When I Am A Vessel launched its educational program in 2018, one thing we observed is that youth had a lot of practical questions about life. Youth are longing for not only relative information but strategies on how to think their way through, and the I Am A Vessel platform is providing them with the resources to do so.

In the next few sections, we've designed a mindset strategy called D-Perspectives, inspired by the character Debo in the movie Friday, written and directed by Ice Cube. Created to give practical examples of how teens and young adults overcome low thinking and living.

D-PERSPECTIVES

D-Perspectives are a set of perspectives designed to empower youth with mindsets that build new outcomes from certain behaviors.

MANY YOUTHS NEED simple examples of how to think themselves through certain circumstances to activate their minds more positively.

Anyone born within this century should know about the movie Friday, written and directed by Ice Cube! But just if someone doesn't....

Debo is a big bully known for not fearing anything. He is rude and ignorant, but we've extracted a positive perspective around his characteristics. The term Debo is also used in urban slang, meaning someone who takes charge. Youth must "Debo" their way beyond low thinking and behaviors.

When youth think from a low posture, they attract below their potential and it can prohibit them from being elevated. Elevation is essentially maturity and promotion into the next level of who they are. Listed below are common distractions challenging the development of today's teens. The purpose is to give teens mental tools (defense) as a collective, to create practical self- empowering mindsets as a standard.

LACK OF FOCUS

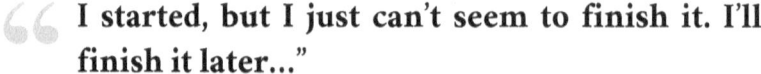 **I started, but I just can't seem to finish it. I'll finish it later..."**

MANY YOUTHS CONFESS that they have **major** challenges being responsible in areas where there are high expectations. Some admit they want to spend their time doing only what they enjoy, meanwhile neglecting priorities, such as completing projects, chores, or even homework.

Some admit to coming home from school and not doing assignments to the point they risk graduating. We're not sure if anyone has **ever** said they absolutely **love** doing homework. However, not doing **any** is a complete waste of time. It just makes logical sense to receive **something** out of learning.

Exactly where does a lack of focus come from? Wherever a person focuses is a sign of what they value. Therefore, youth that **lack** focus may need to put their priorities in order.

Most youths start their day off with their mental capacity already in a deficit. Before they leave their house, energy is wasted on social media, texting, talking on the phone, and other forms of technology; plus, adequate sleep plays a role in this. By the time teens get to school, their energy supply is low or even depleted. This causes teens to be irritable and impatient, which affects their ability to focus and behave.

Each of us has a certain capacity; we can allot each day. Youth must become more aware of how they utilize their daily energy supply. Some may think they lack focus when really, they misuse their energy! Many may even need to create a schedule to learn how they delegate their energy to get things done.

D Perspective- Be stronger than your habits. Master the mind; don't allow the mind to be master over you.

We cannot negate that smartphones play a role in the youth's inability to focus. They must put the smartphones down for second and get connected with themselves. Smartphones can be a **BIG** energy drainer for them. They will have to prioritize on another level, value their mental capacities, and build good habits now! Culture will not create necessary boundaries for them, at least it hasn't yet. Youth should learn the art of focusing, which requires limiting their technology usage.

Getting Woke depends on how well teens prioritize and will sacrifice bad habits to win. When they go off into the world and start their careers, how do youth expect to have the stamina to succeed without the ability to focus. In addition, social media has created a facade that success is easy. One thing it doesn't show youth is that more success means more responsibilities **and** higher expectations. Remember, just like the pyramid, the future is built in layers. It all starts with the ability to focus.

LACK OF MOTIVATION

> **Why do I have to participate in things I don't want to do? I mean, what's the point."**

FOR SOME YOUTH, participation is a challenge that can sometimes frustrate. Many of them underestimate their need to be developed. Motivation is defined as the reasons for acting on something, which ultimately determines the **willingness** to invest in something. At this level, youth should be **highly** motivated because self-investment is the motivation!

Digging deeper into this matter, youth should know, a lack of motivation can reveal their level of maturity. Again, at this level, youth should recognize every opportunity as development for their future. By simply creating a goal, plan, or vision, youth can gain motivation.

Another factor influencing many from being motivated is their ability to self-educate via the internet. Many teens believe that they can self-teach and create their own opportunities. Current culture subliminally has trained youth culture to be unmoved **and** uncommitted because of their ability to see and learn everything instantly. Motivation is sparked by a need! Accessing what they want and when they want it removes the need. The second something gets overwhelming or boring, many youths just move on to the next thing.

Today's culture is motivated by immediate gratification partly due to the access to so much information. The thing is, teens typically need **time** to develop to recognize their personal value, which is discovered when they stick things out. The bigger picture is, lack of motivation can affect teens' ability to self-start and push through to reach their goals.

D Perspectives- Bringing your personal value to everything motivates you!

Rather than wasting energy imagining how pointless something is, rise to the occasion. Youth must realize they don't know how useful anything will be to their futures, so they should learn to be more committed. Every moment is an opportunity to discover themselves. They can only do so when they show up and participate. Utilize new experiences to be beneficial for your personal aspirations. This is what it means to make things happen!

For example, if working in a fast-food restaurant is your current job, and you don't like it. Instead of dreading it every day, use the experience as a training ground for your own future business. So much valuable information is exposed to youth that can be used later in life. For youth working in a fast-food restaurant they should pay attention to the daily flow of business.

As an entrepreneur, they will need to understand problem-solving, inventory, bookkeeping, customer service, and working in a fast pace environment. Recognize, every experience is a set up for the future, and that's motivation always!

CLOUT CHASING

 I need to get my likes up. What should I do?"

SOCIAL MEDIA HAS TAKEN the pressures of popularity to another level. People are stressed out, suffering from anxiety, depression, and anxiousness all over a desire to gain exposure. Over 6.8 billion people own a mobile device, and over 1.4 billion people log onto Facebook. Many youths search daily through social media for inspiration and are influenced by lifestyles they see. Many seek to find a magical formula for popularity to gain validation for their relevancy. Likes and follows are considered assets today!

Social media is a blurred line of reality and fantasy. It's a reality because it is a major component of our everyday life. It's a fantasy because the information gathered is based upon what people want others to know, and not actually how things are. **Perception** is what builds popularity on social media. Status built on perception is being who others expect. Today, even individuals claiming to keep it real are just performing so it garners them the most attention. Popularity and acceptance seem more valuable than genuineness.

Think about it, how silly is it to chase likes, which is just people pretending to approve versions of each other they **think** they know. This desire to have clout translates into many other unhealthy behaviors, and it is the youth's responsibility to create a generational awareness amongst themselves to limit the influence of it **all**!

D Perspective- Spend real-time building true relationships and finding inspiration from tangible connections.

There are many extremely successful, beautiful, and dope people who don't even own a social media account! Youth should do the research to learn the truth about their influencers. Even some celebrities portray themselves differently than they are in real life. The youth must recognize the difference between being entertained and being influenced.

Take time to decipher between the appearance of productiveness and plain ole busyness. Many people on social media **appear** to have it all together to build a reputation and gain followers. Again, youth need a value system within themselves that limits the influence social media has in their lives.

IMPRESSED OR PRESSED?

> **OMG. I love how she looks. That's goals. I'm getting tattoos just like hers. She's lit!"**

THERE ARE SO many options available to youth with minimal guidance on how to decide. Making good decisions is getting more challenging because today, almost anything goes.

Teens are trying out many things and, as a result, are making choices based on trends and because they have free will. Many teens find examples of what's acceptable for themselves on social media. So much is exposed to teens, a green light for them to try out **everything**!

It seems as if they have the free will to participate in everything adults can. There's probably more backlash in judging teens' decisions then boundaries are set for them. If so, how can teens guard themselves so they don't make decisions they will later regret?

CONSIDER.

A great example is choosing a flavor of ice cream from the ice cream shop. It's one thing to choose from a menu of let's say 12 flavors. But what happens when there are over 50 flavors to choose from. How do you decide? When do you decide? How likely is it that you'll be able to narrow the ice cream options down to choose and successfully satisfy your taste buds?

What do you think will happen? Many people would most likely settle or misses the mark. Having so many options can be too much to handle and lessens the chance of making the best choice.

D Perspective- In considering trends and lifestyle choices, teens must think! They should practice the art of good reasoning and weight out the probability of choices before deciding.

Youth should know there are times when they should **try** things and times when they must **decide**! They must know the difference. **Try** new things to help you grow and learn. Measure every decision according to who you want to be. If trying something compromises who you want to be, then **decide** if it's worth it. They should consider that it's easier to welcome a new experience into their lives than it is getting rid of the consequences created because of them.

Remember, a lifestyle is a commitment, and each choice is a doorway leading to more commitments. Choose wisely, and if you ever make a bad choice, simply pay the consequences, redirect yourself and proceed in the right direction!

REAL LIFE DISTRACTED

 **I wish I had a better situation."**

No matter what youth may face, they must understand that challenges are a part of life's journey. They suck! Unfortunately, our circumstances are not always in our control. Thankfully every one of us has the power to overcome anything! We recognize that many youths face challenges every day. No matter what, we are not designed to sit still and let life happen to us.

The process of self-cultivation challenges teens to look ahead and see the bigger picture. Everyone's fighting something, and those who overcome do so because of their ability to focus their energy positively despite circumstances. Each of us has the creative power to survive dysfunction, tragedies, and disappointments.

D Perspective- To the best of their ability, youth should scrutinize within their circumstances to find inspiration and positive power. Wherever there is a need, they should create a space of peace—a space of peace with a plan in mind.

The formula to persevere through challenges has been modeled for us by many great men and women throughout history. The main source of power is in the power of preparation for the future. Knowing who they are despite **any** circumstance allows youth to plan and focus ahead, which gives them the power to position themselves beyond their situations.

The future is **ALWAYS** yours! Youth should make a vision board, research ideas, or even get a mentor to help inspire their aspirations. By implanting vision into their futures, youth can create a way out of anyway.

In conclusion, digging deep is acknowledging that to triumph over every obstacle, teens must sometimes go the extra mile. Digging deep is how every battle is won and how every champion becomes victorious. D Perspectives aims to create a strategy for this key fact of life. Refer to them when needed.

Dig Deep. Grow Strong.

5
EYE SURGERY

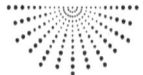

To be the vessels they are, the young generations must see themselves correctly. Their eyes must be set in the correct direction to grab hold of their life's purpose and fulfill the image in which they were created. Youth must learn to go beyond plain sight into their psychological vision. This is SO important!

Vision is the portal to the future! The mere fact that each of us has an innate gift, unique story, and a purpose proves that having a vision is major. Something that youth should think about: If life's purpose has a destination, then the future has a path.

Spiritual vision is the ability to see and feel the unseen to make the right decisions at the right time throughout life's journey. Humanity was not designed to only rely on physical vision; perhaps the eyes are the lesser form of humanity's ability to see. Think about all the types of species and the unique abilities they have within their sight capacities. Species like bats, rhinoceros, and bulls have limited vision and rely greatly on other ways to "see" to survive.

Animals such as owls and eagles are known for their excellent eyesight. As humans, we are equipped with so much. Eyesight, insight, imagination, senses, spirit, and intuition, yet many operate below their capacities. So much development is put into technology and innovation, the same advancement is needed in developing the technology of humanity.

Every few months, Apple launches a new version of the iPhone. Each new model sells out within a few days, making it even more desirable to those who couldn't obtain one. So sleek and shiny when it comes out of the box, it's an amazing feeling, popping open the plastic! Although very few features change from model to model, one feature is usually upgraded... the camera!

The camera may be the most important feature of the iPhone or any smartphone. Capturing ourselves, family, and friends in a crisp manner and in perfect light are so important these days. Especially for platforms like Instagram and YouTube. Different view perspectives, filters, lighting optimization, and advanced video features are all available for those who will make the investment. The caveat is the more humanities ability to see advances through technology, we also tap into different levels of vision.

Our eyes are not only how we see what's in front of us, but are gateways to our minds, hearts, and souls. Generations are being bred in such a visually perfected culture. The question is, how does this reality affect the inner vision?

THE EVOLUTION OF SIGHT

From the moment we are born, we fight to understand how to see things properly to survive. Sight is a gradual process that strengthens from birth to 24 months. We just don't come out and boom we can see! As we grow, we use our sight to understand the world.

The ability to focus our eyes, move them accurately, and use them together must be **learned.** Before we can reach and grab, our eyes provide us with **information and stimulation** important for our **development.**

According to the American Optometric Association, as a baby matures, the hand and eye coordination, judging distances, and depth perception strengthen as the baby becomes mobile. We acquire better eyesight as we crawl. By the time we are walking, we gain interest in **exploring** our environment, which helps us to recognize familiar things and develop other skills such as scribbling with crayons or pencils.

This information is important because as we grow older, we become conscious of other types of lenses we utilize to "see." These sets of lenses also need development, as they help us explore our environments as young teens and adults. Just like a baby, to have a better vision, youth need to see things from different viewpoints.

Viewpoints not in the physical but through the spiritual lenses. Many youths are unaware they utilize their spiritual lenses every second of every minute. The brain processes what it sees at several capacities in which thoughts, feelings, opinions, and emotions are formed. So, with the emotional situations youth go through during maturity, how vital is it for today's youth to develop their spiritual lenses as a resource regarding things such as safety, understanding, and success.

I Am A Vessel has identified 5 innate lenses we use to communicate and navigate through life. These lenses play a critical role in helping youth understand the rollercoaster years of maturation. They are also necessary for the infrastructure of youth development, culture, and humanity.

THE POWER OF THE LENSES

Each lens has a way it functions and influences our mindsets. These lenses can be looked through from a positive viewpoint or a negative one. By learning about them, youth can also learn how to navigate through hard times by channeling their power. They help youth level up their way of thinking.

EVERYONE HAS a set of lenses developed throughout life. Besides these individual lenses, we also create filters for our lenses that seem normal to us. How we process, react, and interact depends on our lenses and filters.

Lenses are like the features on Instagram, that allows users to alter the lighting and coloring of pictures to create a certain focal point. Each of us has lenses with the same ability. Our experiences in life alter our perspectives in different ways, which determines our view. We may even have blind spots because of things we haven't been exposed to. The reason why exploring is so important to self-development.

Maturity requires youth to reset their lenses and remove many old mindsets and habits, and to adopt better outlooks on life to move forward into their next phase. The lenses are influenced by environments, friends, families, circumstances, and situations. Therefore, making healthy decisions and hanging with the right people is critical. People will either enhance your lenses or the exact opposite.

As a beauty expert and creative Visionaire, founder of I Am A Vessel, Sina Marie has changed lives through beauty and creativity. Her unique ability to help individuals through transformational makeover experiences is one attribute she's most known for. Women from all over the country would sit in her styling chair at their most vulnerable times in their lives.

New and old clients each would request she created whatever she wanted with their hair. Sina Marie would be like a mad scientist using every aspect of vision to design something distinctly unique and, most times, out of the comfort zone of the client. She knew that dramatically altering the way her clients saw themselves gave them a fresh perspective of which would create new opportunities for their lives.

Many youths don't realize that their greatest blessing and resource for their future will be the parent, teacher, or friend who gives them the hard truth and pushes them beyond their habits. Because if they don't see the possibilities of who they can be, they may never obtain it. We can only become what we can see and imagine.

Each of Sina Marie's beauty transformations would go beyond the exterior, and her clients would have testimonies of how their lives had been changed. This ability occurs when **foresight** is creatively used as a tool. Here's the great news. We each can do this for ourselves when we use our **insigh**t and operate from the inside out! This is a daily strategy for life. The right vision will change your life!

THE TECHNOLOGY OF VISION

The 5 Vessel Lenses

The technology of humanity's vision is even more advanced than our own understanding. Humans can see with the eyes, ears, heart, mind, soul, and intuition. We believe these are foundational pillars of every Vessel.

Here are the 5 Vessel Lenses, which are forms of sight we use to see beyond the eyes. They are each connected to different aspects of our minds.

- *PERSPECTIVE* - The part of sight connected to our experiences and expectations.

- *IMAGINATION* - The part of sight connected to the

Divine power within that includes our innate and supernatural ability to create. It is also the gateway to our past, present, and most importantly, the future.

- *Beauty* - The part of sight connected to our ideals, values, and inspiration.

- *Knowledge* - The part of sight that connects all life and purpose.

- *Cultural* - It is a subconscious form of sight. The part of sight that shifts and changes according to the present mentality of society and community.

The Perspective lens is how we view life itself. Our perspective is shaped by our experiences, upbringings, lifestyle, beliefs, and things of this nature. It changes as we evolve. Looking at our perspective reminds us to continually renew our minds and evolve into better thinkers because whether teens realize or not, they set boundaries on themselves based on their life experiences.

A healthy perspective depends on teens' ability to be flexible in their thinking, discover new environments, and develop relationships that broaden their view—a critical factor for inner growth.

Its POWER
The right perspective can neutralize a negative into a positive. This lens is a great source of our inner healing. Understand how powerful

> this is. Our minds are to be used to evolve us.
> Teens must learn to use this neutralizing
> power to their advantage as they get out into
> the real world. They must challenge their
> thinking in negative situations to find
> whatever piece of power they can. Teens are
> the future leaders and should relentlessly
> develop mature perspectives.

The *Imagination* lens is our individual inner creativity and a pathway to our higher self. To create anything, we must use our imagination. Whatever can be imagined can be created! When youth acknowledge, write, or articulate what they imagine, it becomes a vision. A vision with a plan becomes achievable. There's nothing more powerful than when visions become businesses, accomplishments, art, and dreams fulfilled. When we use the innate tools within our imaginations, it connects us to a higher source where we can capture anything that we need to create.

Our personality is connected to the nature of our imagination. Both are key to discovering who we are. Many people have said jokingly, "I don't have a creative bone in my body." However, if they put effort into seeking their imaginations and exploring themselves within, they will discover their creative abilities and so much more.

> ### Its POWER
> Some youth today think using their imaginations
> is silly and a waste of time. It is troubling
> that many are impatient to grow up to
> become adults, because their greatness is

discovered when they creatively explore within. Imagination is humanity's connection to the spiritual realm, which is where our inspirations and desires can be tapped into and produced.

It is our connection, a pathway to a higher power, and our higher intelligence as it gives us the capability to turn nothing into something! When we captured the unseen things and used them to produce the tangible, we are operating by design. Imagination is the vehicle for all of humanity to discover who they are and re-produce from the posture of being living vessels.

The *Beauty* **lens is linked to our ideals and values.** Beauty is the value we see in something. If something catches your eyes and you think it's beautiful, then there's a quality in it you value.

Beauty represents not only what we value, but the **substance** of value based on our inner beliefs. Our personalities, confidence, upbringings, experiences, and things of that nature. Beauty has many layers to it. We often equate something that's appealing to being beautiful.

> **True beauty inspires us to look beyond exterior stimulations to find the unique quality of something that awakens and can transform us."**

— SINA MARIE

A great imagery is the butterfly, one of the universal symbols of beauty. The metamorphosis of a caterpillar to a butterfly is a great example of the depth of beauty—the caterpillar making its way to becoming a butterfly so it may be free. The stages of the process are left with physical evidence of its transformation, the shedding of its skin.

There is beauty in the struggle! Beauty inspires us to self-discovery and reveals to us the purpose of the process. Something is beautiful when it has overcome, survived, or started small and became big.

To sum it up, beauty is a quality that can be understood through the story of transformation and the residuals of its aftermath. Love, respect, peace, joy, and inspiration are beautiful even more so when we discover them after being denied or void of them. Therefore, it becomes priceless and valued.

> ### Its **POWER**
> *When we find the beauty in all things, we are led to find it first within. Beauty motivates and shapes us to become the highest version our ourselves. When we experience loss, trials, and tribulations and are restored through the journey of seeking deeply within, we gain strength, fortitude, and respect for who we are.*

*A relating fact about beauty---Webster dictionary

defines beauty as the qualities in a person or things that give pleasure to senses or exalts the mind or spirit.

The *Knowledge* lens familiarizes us with who we are as individuals and as a collective. Knowledge of self is the goal we are all searching for. It can't be acquired by the outside world but through the world inside each of us. It is our divine connection to creation. The more youth read, research, participate, study, explore and inquire information, a mystical pathway is revealed, leading to their greatest potential. If teens want to know how amazing they are, they must press through the pathway of knowledge.

Anything you want to change about yourself or life, you must become knowledgeable about it. If you want to change your circumstances, you must become knowledgeable. To break a record, you must become knowledgeable of how it was done the first time. Knowledge is also obtained through mentors, researching, studying, testing, searching, questioning, and asking. (So, you can imagine the consequences of thinking you know everything.)

The definition of knowledge supports this theory. Wikipedia defines knowledge as familiarity, awareness, or understanding of someone or something, such as facts, information, descriptions, or skills, which is acquired through the experience or education of perceiving, discovering, or learning.

Its POWER
Knowledge is key to finding purpose. It is an exploration that leads youth to awaken an

inner understanding of who they are. Information learned resonates and expands youths' minds, each in different ways--- unveiling interests that reveals what's hidden inside of them. If youth want to continually grow and elevate, they should never stop learning and educating themselves. Knowledge activates the creative process. The power of words is the smallest form of humanity's ability in manifestation.

In other words, our thoughts are not tangible, but when they become words, they began to physically structure our lives, ideas, hopes, and dreams. Whatever you may be curious about for your future, go research it. Something is amazing, waiting to be revealed to you.

THE *CULTURAL LENS* **is our sociological lens that determines how we connect with one another.** It is a lens that changes or is reshaped throughout time. The current cultural lens of today is shaped greatly by social media and technology. Perhaps it can be considered an artificial lens, so to speak. It has become a lens through which we seek validation or acceptance. Social media is a free advertisement for everyone to promote themselves. The more likes and follows a person have, the more "approved" they are considered. The downside of this self-promotion is it can leave youth and adults feeling unworthy and rejected.

Social media is not a natural lens of life. However, it has a power of influence or *reactive power*. It does not hold *true power*. True power is a natural power. It comes from within. There is a distinction between something **being** powerful and something **having** power. What *is...*, can't be taken away; and what *has...*, can be taken away. Individuality **is** power. Youth culture has power. The benefits of its power can only be activated and utilized according to the level of understanding youth have.

Youth culture must have a deeper comprehension of what's happening around them, good and bad, to utilize its power. Knowing the underlying factors of social media is crucial to the mental sustainability of today's youth—social media influences how the youth see themselves and others. Many teens don't realize that perhaps their very own thoughts and opinions aren't their own but are the residuals of other peoples.

Some of their sensory responses are influenced by social media and have become embedded in their mind frames. It's time for teens to look beyond what's in front and learn of everything happening around them.

> ### I<small>TS</small> POWER
> *Social media is a false sense of inner power.*
> > *Here's the thing about true power, no one can take it away. If social media shuts down, how powerful would some people be? However, social media is the power of influence. Influence is important in culture. The thing*

is, there are negative and positive influences. If used positively, influence can be a powerful source. Morals and good intentions ultimately determine the direction in which the lens of social media is channeled.

CONSIDER.

The concern for the culture is that if social media determines the standard for youth culture, then what does this mean the culture is built on?

6
LEVEL UP

IT'S A FEW WAVES OUT HERE IN THE CULTURE THAT EVERYONE IS on, and a notable wave is the "level up." Everyone wants to level up. What exactly does it mean to level up?

The dictionary defines level up as a phrasal verb meaning to progress to the next level or advance one's character to the next level. What needs to take place to make leveling up possible for many youths?

To level up, we think youth must go beyond the surface and dissect the way they think and speak. So much of who they are is shaped by their thoughts. During the maturity years, youth spend a lot of time in their heads, thinking many thoughts, which is why the mindset of teens is so important.

This is mandatory to consider because the prominence that words and thoughts have in the human experience is undeniable. We will explore the dynamics of words and thoughts and the role they play into the development and prosperity of today's youth.

ME, MYSELF, AND I

Beyoncé has a song titled me, myself, and I. In the lyrics, she states, in the end, all she has is herself. At the end of the hook, she decides she would be her own best friend. Although, realistically, we need people, it's something to think about. If you had to be your own best friend... would you? If you could experience yourself as another person does, would you stick around?

What makes someone a good friend? A person's character and personality play a big role in determining if so or not. Many people have a great personality and not so great characters. Personality is defined as the outward appearance or behavior of a person like their image, public relations skills, and communication skills. A lot of relationships are built on whether a person has an appealing personality.

While character refers to a set of morals, mental qualities, and beliefs of a person. The actual traits of a person are hidden from sight. Both personality and character will need revamping throughout life. No one should spend their entire life looking or behaving the same as they did as adolescence. However, many people never take the time to redesign who they are. One of the easiest ways to level up is to change one's personality, but what if someone seeks to change profoundly? When people want to become successful, they look deeper into who they are.

When we talk about building ourselves from the inside out, we are referring to the structural components of your inner mind and spirit. Ask yourself, what are the components inside of you? Maybe you have never thought about the significance of defining yourself, now is the time!

As a man thinketh in his heart so is he"

PROVERBS 23:7

THE POWER OF WORDS AND THOUGHTS

Becoming strong from the inside out can be a lifelong journey, but with a clear understanding of the power of words and thoughts, youth can expedite the process. The power of words is **real**. Youth should know their words shape their reality. The words they choose reflects what's in their heart. Speaking positively gives youth inner power, which creates an outer world hard to be defeated. From the music they listen to the hashtags they use on social media, these things all play a major role in youth lives.

The Human Engineering Lab studied thousands of successful people to see if they could identify success traits. Studies show that it is not a person's upbringing, it is not where they live or even their social background that determines the probability of success. The one thing that successful people have in common is a large vocabulary. Yup. That's it. A strong vocabulary is necessary to develop and self-cultivate.

CONSIDER.

People with a large vocabulary, do they normally suffer from low self-confidence?

Are they usually afraid to speak and communicate?

ExecuComm Inc., the owner of the trademark, **Power Words**, defines the term as words that empower people to communicate at a higher level. Believe it or not, words have the power to provoke you to do things. For instance, if someone called a girl beautiful, she might walk around all day feeling like she's that girl! Why? Because words have the power to change our mindsets instantly!

Rice Experiment:

Dr. Masaru Emoto is a researcher of water, famous for experimenting with the magic of water, also known as the rice experiment. During this experiment, Dr. Emote exposed music, spoken words, typed words, pictures, and videos to water. After the water was crystalized, what he found under the microscope was astonishing.

The water exposed to positive messages of love and peace formed beautiful crystals, each different depending on the word or sound they were exposed to. The water exposed to negative input yielded the opposite result. Now, there were other questionable factors involved, such as the location from which the water came. Still, overall the experiment inspired others to do their own tests. People all over the world redid this experiment using rice submerged in water.

The experiment involved three containers. Each container was labeled one of the following, love, hate, or ignore. Thoughts and words were communicated to each container according to its label. In addition, each container had descriptions of additional words and thoughts on their matching labels. These words and thoughts were meditated and spoken over each for the 30 days. The results were consistent according to reports.

First and foremost, this experiment demonstrates how powerful water and sound is! Sound is energy created by vibration. We could think of this on many levels. Vibration can be measures of intention, mood, etc. because they each create a dimension of sound that's felt. The experiment also shows how critical labeling can be to developing people.

How the experiment works:

Water, which is found to carry energy, is absorbed by the rice. The rice is influenced by the vibration created from the words.

What people discovered was the rice was stable in the container labeled love; it became moldy and distorted in the container labeled hate; the container labeled ignore resulted in unpredictable and varied results. Which is worst, the negative label or the ignore label? As you can see, ignoring things also has a negative effect.

Consider.

80 percent of the human body is made of water. If water carries energy through our body in response to our thoughts and words, then how youth talk and think is more important than they may know. Experts estimate we think 60,000-80,000 thoughts per day! That's an average of 2,500-3,300 thoughts per hour! Youth must posture their words with positive attitudes because it has physical effects on their minds and bodies!

I HATE EVERYTHING!

How often have you felt like you just hated everything! This sounds dramatic, but so many emotions youth feel are normal. Normal, but not meant to stagnate their growth. If youth are not careful, they can allow negative thoughts and behaviors to shape their relationships and environments.

Some youth go through a phase where they draw negative situations to themselves because it seems easier to **speak** negatively versus shifting their minds in a positive direction. However, it's never too late to mature and redirect things.

In addition to the power of their words, youth must explore their thinking, which cannot be explored without considering their emotional capacities.

You know when someone says a person is not on their level, they mean that person is not matured enough to understand how to react or respond correctly to a situation.

Immaturity can cause youth to be emotionally unbalanced. They can either be overly sensitive or on the extreme opposite and **just don't care**! Which is why maturity also affects judgment. Until they learn to balance their emotions, youth may decide based solely on how they **feel** about something. It's just too shaky to decide based on emotions!

Ask yourselves these questions. How do I respond to situations? Am I easily upset **or**, should I care more about how others feel? This is important because to be effective in their aspirations, youth must know how to properly respond.

Youth today need to know that in the real world, they must be self-aware and possess the right attitudes to prosper. Many images in media today have given youth false expectations that ill attitudes and bad behaviors will reap the good benefits. This is just not a reality.

One of the hardest lessons everyone must learn is that the world does not revolve around them! A big part of respecting this reality is knowing that we all want the same things, love and happiness!

MATURITY CHANNELS

Maturity channels represent the two emotional aspects of our humanity, our spiritual and carnal selves.

BESIDES DEALING with adolescence and the process of maturation, there are two things youth should become more aware of about themselves. Youth could mentally be at ease, knowing they are not only carnal beings but spiritual ones. Emotional balance happens when they allow themselves to be both spiritual and carnal.

Realize that some days you can be emotionally off balance and need to rest even and take time off from too much stimulation. Negative attitudes sometimes arise because of feeling overwhelmed spiritually and not allowing time to get emotionally balanced. Again, this is all-natural. Could some ill behaviors be because of merely needing space and time to regroup?

Some situations that occur during the adolescent years are just lessons trying to teach youth to pay closer attention to their inner needs. They spend more time learning how to master themselves carnally, they may not understand this spiritual need. It's time for society to recognize youth have deep emotional needs and to put more emphasis not only on mental but spiritual wellness.

Although young, they are also on a journey towards discovery, healing, and ultimately self-actualization. These are the years where youth should spend adequate time being quiet, contacting their inner voice, and training their minds to respond positively to life's situations. Which is key to **Self-Unity™**, an I Am A Vessel term that describes when your spirit, mind and soul agree with one another.

Think of a toddler who cries to get his or her way. The baby has to learn to ask and wait patiently to be given what he or she wants. To develop a baby's aptitude for a new level of response, parents must build the baby's inner ability to practice self-control by challenging the baby's old carnal reactions. It takes a while, but once a toddler realizes there is a new level of resistance, he or she must make the needed adjustments.

Instead of screaming for what he/she wants, babies eventually learn better ways to respond and communicate. Imagine how frustrating the feeling of resistance is to a baby. Especially since they cannot talk effectively. Resistance is a **big** part of developing our maturity channels.

TRIPPING' OR NAW...

Many youths admit they need to work on their attitudes. As we mentioned, growing up is an emotional rollercoaster that stems from youth trying to understand where to fit within the collective. The Vessel pyramid is a symbol that we each are dimensionally created: within ourselves, families, community/world. We all have more than one role to play, which requires us to effectively communicate.

At different stages in life, we fluctuate between being **emotional or detached**. Sometimes it can seem as if the right attitude is unachievable!

Studies have shown that people who operate from their emotions are loving and caring individuals. On the flip side, they are also overly sensitive and impulsive in decision making. Emotional people take everything to heart and view things deeper than others. Does this sound like you?

On the opposite side, people who operate based on logistics and facts use mind over the heart in responding in situations. Others may feel they lack compassion. Logical individuals underestimate the benefits of deep emotional connections. They sometimes may lack the vision to see beyond what's in front. Or is this you?

Here's the deal, when youth decide they want to fulfill the role they play in their own lives, families, and communities, they are forced to find a balance to communicate effectively with others. The Vessel pyramid teaches us we must strengthen and build ourselves up. Then we can expand out and take our place to become a part of something bigger! Our mental and emotional intelligence will need to be balanced.

Keep Calm.
There is a Strategy.

THE BALANCE BEAM THEORY

How can teens learn to balance between being logical and emotional? Think about the balance beam competition in which an athlete maintains balance to perform gymnastic techniques. This is an example of what life feels like sometimes!

The website **usagym.org** outlines the strategies necessary for a gymnast to balance on a balance beam. The key components are **posture, alignment, strength, and control**. These are great strategies for youth to develop healthy attitudes, build character, and structure their mindsets. They should use them to function maturely in relationships and situations.

Why is balance significant to youth emotionally and mentally leveling up? It takes operating both emotional and logical characteristics of who they are to navigate in relationships and atmospheres effectively.

The objective of these strategies is to give youth practical tools to move beyond lower-level behaviors that stop them from operating in their greatness.

POSTURE

Posture secures position.

THE RIGHT ATTITUDE is key to developing the emotional maturity needed to build good relationships, both personal and business. Many youths have a sense of entitlement and have not learned how to adapt their attitudes when necessary. This might sound brash; however, an attitude of humility goes a long way; youth should adopt the posture/attitude that the world doesn't revolve around them.

Of course, still maintain confidence. Having this posture of confidence and humility takes a lot of will, especially in today's world, when culture teaches youth to have an "it's all about me attitude." However, a mature youth recognizes there are great rewards for demonstrating humility.

ALIGNMENT

Attitude and energy align with moments

ALIGN the right energy and attitude at the right moment. Just like the balance beam, every moment counts and requires certain moves. Youth should learn to discern how and when to react. Knowing when to speak up and be quiet is a skill set that develops as youth learn who they are. It is a product of maturation. Always be yourself, but learning the art of the moment is easier when youth learn to balance their emotional energy.

STRENGTH

Vulnerability is strength

SOME TEENS ARE SO PREDICTABLE. Like clockwork, everyone knows what response they will give in certain situations. They must learn to maturely communicate, which may require some youth to adopt a new way of responding. Anyone who is past the age of learning to tie their shoes should know how to operate in order and authority. Surrendering to authority can feel vulnerable, and for many, it may literally be painful to follow instructions.

However, looking into the future, youth that are willing to be vulnerable and adjust their attitudes will create pathways towards success. Some youth struggle with their attitudes and behaviors; they should realize that one decision to become compliant can eliminate so many other unnecessary issues when they activate this aspect of strength.

CONTROL

Self-control is a weapon of wisdom

TEENS MUST PRACTICE SELF-CONTROL! Reacting on an impulse will keep teens stagnant, and **frankly,** as they get older, people won't tolerate it. Imagine if students took education as a serious developmental process and practiced good posture, alignment, strength, and control—behaviors that would assist them in studying, paying attention, and building sound relationships with others.

How many other issues would students avoid or solve? Imagine also if teens found better ways to express their anger, frustration, or attitude in general? How quickly would they advance by attracting more positive energy, people, and opportunities to their lives? When youth give themselves the space to grow emotionally, they change their inner **and** outer world drastically and become drivers and not passengers in their own lives. When youth activate wisdom, they become conquerors and not victims of their circumstances.

7
NO LIMITS

WE HOPE ANY YOUTH, TEEN, OR YOUNG ADULT WHO READS THIS information realize that they have more power to develop themselves with intention and that it is their responsibility to do so. Much of the inner turmoil or confusion they may feel is a part of maturing. The reality is that teens must be kind, gentle, and forgiving to themselves as they develop. They also must be knowledgeable, strategic, aware, and irrevocably purposed.

BREAKING LIMITATIONS

A lot of us have endured many things in our lives. However, maturation is key to empower beyond the residuals of circumstances—maturity positions you to move ahead of limitations. The way youth unplug themselves from past constraints are by the daily renewing of their minds. Bringing their focus and thoughts in alignment to looking beyond their circumstances, which allows them to gain momentum towards the future. A changed mind is powerful!

It is very possible for any youth who wants to be better or stronger to go to sleep one night and awaken a new person because of a renewed commitment to their future.

Hip Hop mogul Master P called himself a "No limit Soldier," which is also the name of his record label. His lyrics state," I'm a no-limit soldier... I thought I told ya!" This is a powerful set of statements. First, he declared to *himself* who he was; and then he declared to the doubters by saying, "I thought I told ya"! Many youths need to say to negative thoughts and people... "I thought I told ya!"

His mindset is the reason he made history by starting the first independent record label in hip hop culture. When he decided he wanted better, he used the power of words with a changed mind. With an intentional set of values, he applies them to climb his way up to success! Because he changed his mindset, he created generational wealth for his family and made history!

Everyone wants to make history, but are they willing to do the work? History makers aren't afraid to be different. In culture today, it's easy to use looks, designer clothes, plastic surgery, other people's ideas, and exterior things to gain applause. **In the end, what history is being made? What will people remember you by?**

This segment is dedicated to Master P and his historical accomplishments as they are an example for future generations. Besides the fact he demonstrated courage and persistence, he used his words, mind, and actions to become great. He intentionally operated by design!

As one final clean sweep, let's examine collective behaviors within youth culture that are limitations, and let's set the bar for breaking through.

ACCESS DENIED

What would happen if, for no apparent reason, someone stepped to you on your way to school or work and tells you they want to fight you? They say the reason is that you simply think your "all of that." Although this seems absurd, it happens.

Here, some youth wouldn't hesitate and jump into a full-fledge fight off the rip! The second someone even looks at them wrong, they are ready for a royal rumble!

Self-defense comes naturally to most. It is a natural instinct to protect ourselves from harm in whatever way we feel strong enough to do. There are many other ways youth need to get tough and learn to protect themselves.

CONSIDER.

It's one thing to fight a person, but how about negative thoughts that invade our minds daily? What's the attitude or the response when confronted in this capacity? How tough are you when a negative thought keeps you from being your best? How strong are you mentally?

Isn't it equally important for youth to protect their minds as they would protect their reputations or their space! Even a toddler understands the importance of protecting their space. Small children are very territorial and are serious about who they allow into their personal realm. It's just an instinctive behavior of theirs. A toddler will push someone to create a physical barrier within their personal proximities.

The question becomes, why aren't we instinctive about protecting ourselves from negative thoughts? Perhaps because the brain naturally processes information, good and bad, we just assume negative thoughts have access to our minds? However, as a toddler pushes away or denies certain people from having access to them, it is the same protection youth must learn to have over negative thoughts to their minds.

Negativity is a residual matter from bad experiences, insecurities, ill energies, and flawed traits within. Youth must learn to demonstrate authority over it. Let's look at some limitations affecting youth culture and then strategize how to deny access to them.

COMMON LIMITATIONS

Common-law marriage is when individuals operate as if they're married but have not undergone the process legally.

MARRIAGE IS a covenant agreement between two individuals in spirit and in the flesh, which makes marriage vows a sacred decree. Just like a marriage between two people, many youths may not realize this. Still, they make covenants with themselves through certain words and thoughts. Covenants that shape who they are because words have power.

Concerning common law marriage, individuals have limited legal rights despite how long they've been together. Legally married individuals are protected by law and granted certain rights with a divorce. This term and example of common law marriages is a creative perspective we are using to describe how some youth operate in a covenant with opinions and behaviors that are not a complete or true representation of who they are.

For example, when a teen is used to identify as the bad girl or the quiet guy, they may wish to change, but they don't; sometimes, teens continue to project behaviors that maintain the approval and expectations of others.

CONSIDER.

What thoughts and behaviors are limiting your full potential? Who might you be if you separate yourself from the belief system you currently operate with?

Are you used to conducting yourself a certain way based on common expectations placed on you?

How many youths you know have common-law relationships with self- imposed limiting behaviors? They view themselves negatively by habit or repute.

For example, when the prettiest girl ever may think she's unattractive, or a guy is a bully because he is unhappy with himself. It works both ways.

Many of the limited opinions youth place on themselves result from an experience of something being done or said to them that negatively affected their self-image. These experiences can cause teens to develop opinions of themselves that affect the way they interact with others and vice versa.

In other instances, many teens who are brilliant and unique and who may not "fit in with the crowd" may not appreciate their uniqueness. Often these individuals will build relationships in circles they don't belong in and must change who they are to stay connected. This is an example of how many smart individuals end up on the wrong path in life.

Many youths want to know how to break through these limitations. They want to see themselves strong, beautiful, smart, but their inner turmoil is a battle of self- acceptance, and esteem—a battle all may encountered at one time or another, which there is no quick fix. However, by making a covenant with new thoughts, behaviors, outlooks, they can break free.

Let's step towards becoming no limit soldiers like Master P. Step one is facing things head-on, so we must address a few things.

It's time for many youths to stop focusing so deeply on others."

SINA MARIE

NEGATIVE SELF IMAGE

A negative self-image can manifest, such as an inferiority complex and sometimes even shyness.

NEGATIVE COMPLEXES CAN DEVELOP when the youth constantly compare themselves to others. The dreadful habit of comparison is one mindset that will creep up if youth are not self-aware. A comparison will have them base their self-value on the strength or popularity of their peers.

This outlook is silly when you actually think about it. The root of it stems from admiration, which is positive. But if not careful, admiration can turn into envy if one is too focused on others and not enough on oneself.

Especially because it can cause youth to believe untrue things about themselves. They can become fearful about being disliked and constantly self-ridicule. A good number of adults have spent a portion of their adolescence in this zone. Youth should avoid focusing so deeply on others and spend more time appreciating who they are. By not seeking validation, they can have a vision for their own unique qualities.

Now, this isn't an easy perspective to adopt, especially when current culture indirectly advertises validation through likes, follows, and comments.

Counter to culture, self-value is most important. Focusing on how others see you puts too much personal power into the opinions of others.

CONSIDER**.**

People will inconsistently change their temperament towards you every day! Logically, how much sense does it make to depend on other people's opinions to feel worthy?

No one is perfect, and everyone should be working on loving themselves more. Any youth who struggle with a negative self-image has to first search within themselves. They should look to find any changes they may make **within**, to better the way they see themselves, which helps to change how they feel **inside**.

Youth can gain a positive outlook of themselves by building a strong self-identity, which starts by defining who they are. Definition brings more clarity, necessary for a healthy relationship with oneself.

It's difficult to define themselves if they are constantly viewing the lives of others on social media. Youth should limit their time on social media as it can be a distraction from getting grounded within. Building self-confidence and appreciation for themselves is much easier without the daily interference of comparing and contrasting the lives of others.

ARROGANCE AND EGOTISMS

Self-Advocacy is wonderful, but balance is key.

SOME SAY that true confidence is quiet. For clarification, confidence and arrogance are different and should not be confused. Real confidence doesn't need a squad or a cosign to back it up. Beneath it all, arrogance is connected to the fear of rejection and inadequacy, especially if a person longs to be admired and respected.

Acknowledging that other people are dope too, is a sign of a matured ego. Everyone has an ego, and it should never be turned off. Still, one's ego should not fight to overpower every other ego; it comes into contact with. Youth must learn how to communicate with others while accepting that everyone may not think they're the greatest.

This posture teaches youth to care less about what others think and promotes a healthy ego. Make it a habit to see great things in others and fight the need to always be the center of attention!

Yes, we are **boldly** confronting self- limiting behaviors because we live in a culture that creates circumstances that develop them. A bright future requires a balanced ego, and many youths need to develop one now!

CLEANING UP THE PERCEPTION

Spiritual excellence is thinking the highest thoughts of oneself and others. It is a term I Am A Vessel coined to give teens a perspective to reference to break self-limited thoughts and behaviors. Demonstrating spiritual excellence is a tool to defuse egotistical behavior and even self-judgment. It can be a method to help balance the inner turmoil youth may have when trying to assert or reserve themselves.

By always working towards thinking the highest thoughts, youth can develop the ability to positively engage with others. Engaging during the maturity years can be tricky! Teens either like or dislike one another. However, this results from immaturity. There is such a thing as levels of engagement. Everyone has value, so turning one another off is not a reflection of how things work in the real world.

Practicing spiritual excellence is a game-changer for life because it will train youth to recognize the value of people beyond their outer exteriors. A small adjustment in behavior that can prepare youth for the unexpected person they may meet on an airplane one day, who could change their lives!

UNAWARE OR DON'T CARE

Knowledge of one's own character, feelings, motives, beliefs, and desires is the remedy for common self-limiting behaviors.

How important is self-awareness? Self-awareness is a strength everyone should operate in. Many youths don't because they refuse to engage with themselves seriously. They can be preoccupied with friendships, school work, and activities. They may not invest enough time becoming familiar with who they are. Which is a form of blindness? No one can be secure in any situation where they have limited understanding, especially about themselves.

Self- Awareness Is Empowerment That Shuts Down Limitations.

AUTHENTICITY BEGINS HERE! The more youth know about themselves, the more they value who they are. Knowing the full spectrum of themselves, the good **and** the bad is powerful. Strengths and weaknesses are there for a reason, and people who try to deny them in some ways are blind to certain aspects of themselves. For many, self-awareness is a life long journey, but this book is a powerful tool giving teens the knowledge on how to expedite the process! Self-awareness is how to reach **true** inner power!

Self-Acceptance is Under-Rated

WE HEAR SO MUCH about people keeping it real. But social media displays things differently. Why do people work so hard at being genuine and keeping things "100" with others, but often we find they aren't real with themselves?

Self- acceptance is being comfortable with one's uniqueness. Youth can be empowered when they honor who they are **not**! Which shouldn't be considered a shortcoming because nobody has it all!

Today many people will pay for what they rarely possess. Plastic surgery has become a trend for women to undergo the knife to gain popularity and fame. Individuals completely physically change who they are to love themselves. Still, no matter how much surgery, fame, attention a person buys, true confidence is an inside and not an outside job.

SCARED OR NAW?

Apprehension can be fear in disguise.

STRONG APPREHENSION REGARDING TRYING new things can be fear disguised. The fear of starting something new, being misunderstood, being accepted, being alone, speaking up, meeting new people, learning, sharing, and believing in yourself will hamper your ability to discover where you belong. Being a Vessel isn't just cultivating yourselves but also finding where your abilities can flourish. This is a form of self-love!

Many youths let fear stop them from growing or even winning! **Just do it!** The Nike mindset is one to adopt with fear regarding your self-development. Caution is an important practice, but in developing themselves to the next level, youth should be open to new opportunities that help them grow.

Fear should be replaced by confidence. Boost confidence by gaining knowledge. Learning gives youth the confidence to not only move forward but complete things they start. So, if youth feel the urge to procrastinate or make excuses, they should research, practice, and become knowledgeable to remove anxiety or fear.

CONSIDER

- How hard are you on yourself to be perfect to be accepted by others?

- How far have you gone out of your way to being accepted or how closed off have you become because of the fear of rejection?

- Can you honestly say you operate as your true self, or are you trying to find yourself in others?

Many of the common limitations teens experience result from teens trying to identify the root of who they are, a process every human must go through.

Vessel of the Future
(n): a game changer, a problem solver, a visionary for the future

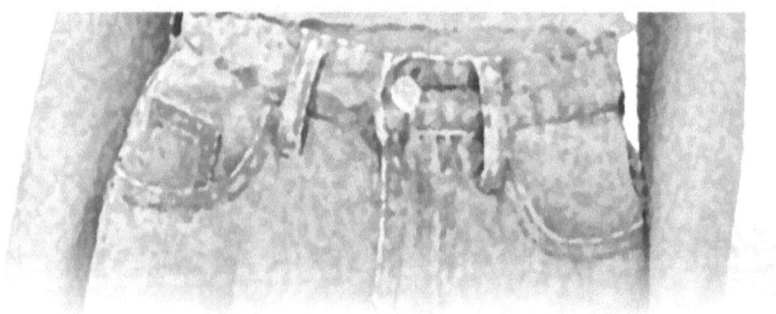

MINDSET IS LEGACY

If we look at the life of Master P, as he is a living legacy, there are a few things we can observe. He is proof and an example of how we are to build our lives. Youth can look at Percy Miller's history and learn how he turned his name into a legacy. Whatever you call yourself should reflect what you want to become.

Naming himself **Master** P, demonstrated that he envisioned himself being powerful and living life on his own terms. He exemplified discipline, which further aligned with his goal of being not a slave to anyone or anything, but the master over his future. He lived up to this name. In the 1990s, Master P was offered a major record deal in which he turned down a million dollars because he wanted to maintain ownership over his name and music.

He decided if he wanted to be the main beneficiary of his brand, he would have to have the faith that a better opportunity would happen, or he would make one! That's what he did! Master P. did the research and turned what little he had into something. He landed a major distribution deal that gave him a $375,000 advance, ownership over all of his music, his name, and 75% of the wholesale price over every record sold—a deal unheard of.

Master P proved himself to be a master of his life and a **No Limit Soldier!** He was one of the first rap artists to turn his career into multiple million-dollar businesses. Everything from music, movies, real estate, clothing, high-end travel agency, video game company, and many others. Still today, Master P is the fifth wealthiest rap artist in the world! This is sure proof that wealth is a mindset.

YOUTH DOMINION

Dominion means to have sovereignty or control over a territory.

AS WE UNLOCKED new levels of understanding, it is the objective for youth to understand the mandate of dominion over their lives and futures.

It is also where the term domain comes from for those who may have a website. It is the space that one governs and has the authority to decide what goes on. Our perspective, youth dominion is about taking charge and responding to things that affect youth culture versus adapting to them.

But to also become investigators by looking around themselves for the revealing of the information and opportunity to demonstrate wisdom. Knowledge moves youth beyond being impressed by the mundane.

Dominion is a leadership term exemplified in the Bible initially. When youth think in terms of having dominion, then they discover ways to lead and not follow. Youth should shift and elevate their minds to see beyond instant or easy pursuits. They could benefit from seeing themselves creating social media platforms focusing on building the culture.

Rather than spending endless hours perhaps plotting on becoming social media famous.

Being a Vessel is about leading the way for others towards something. We are all designed to be Vessels. To shape and build our lives so we may serve a great purpose within the fullness of life, our families, and communities.

8
LET THERE BE LIGHT

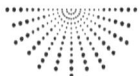

THIS LAST PORTION OF *GET WOKE* WILL SOLIDIFY OUR EFFORTS to recalibrate and effectively ascend youth in their development into adulthood and a deeper understanding of the times we live in. Synonymous with restoring the value of the intellectual capacities of youth culture.

The purpose of this intense journey of excavating through real topics is so youth see the role they play to live complete, healthy, and happy on higher levels. Young women and men should know today they can start fresh and redirect their focus so they can discover more about who they are.

I Am A Vessel hopes that digging into topics such as information overload, technology, social media, threats to youth identities and **spiritual ecosystems** has sparked a continued conversation amongst not only youth but all those connected to them. It is our best intentions this information has pushed individuals past any insecurity, stigmatization, negative outlook, self- pity, stagnant mentalities, culture façade, and any systemic boundary that challenges their abilities to spiritually and mentally thrive.

Even with learning all the information we've shared, it's necessary to provide a solid method for youth to put everything they've learned into action.

STRATEGY

Many youths may lack the understanding of how to put the work in to move to their next level. Some get stuck because they may lack the vision to see beyond where they are. How are youth supposed to gain the confidence to take healthy risks which teach them to overcome obstacles in a profound way?

As mentioned earlier, they need a **belief system** with enough substance to equip them with the fortitude to move beyond what they see and sometimes experience. Activities such as joining a sports team is a great way to activate confidence, but many challenges the current culture face requires a high level of resilience. A complex culture **needs** deeper knowledge, real substance, and revelation.

Moving beyond limitations amongst the youth of today needs an active dose of faith. What is faith? To put it plainly, faith is the confidence to believe the highest outcome for something that may not appear to be or ever become available to you. Many people face circumstances that reflect the need for faith.

Healing, freedom, and resources are examples of things that require many people to activate their faith. The ability to have faith for something is often fueled by a thought, feeling, or desire better on the other side. It is the currency for fortitude and resilience.

Revelation gives humanity strategy in decision making, planning, and structuring our lives. It is an intuitive understanding of who we are and why we are here. It has the power to redirect our thoughts and activate our path throughout the process of discovering. Youth should know that the inner feeling they have about the greatness inside of them is more than a "gut" feeling. That feeling deep down inside means something, and they must act on it because it's leading them somewhere amazing!

While revelation is necessary, youth also need practical strategies that speak to the culture of today. It's important to know every new level of life requires a new strategy, and it will always begin in the mind.

YOUTH INTELLIGENCE

As we enter into a new era. An era of acceleration happening in all areas of humanity. A systematic approach is applied to everything. What does this mean? Youth should be aware that everything is based upon a set of objectives and should observe what's presented to them dimensionally. They must be able to look beyond what's directly in front of them! Using their insight, youth can recognize the dynamics within these systems that tap into their minds, daily lives, and futures in ways not healthy for them.

Practicing the discerning intelligence that they naturally

possess is imperative. An intelligence activated and strengthened the more they acknowledge their spiritual attributes. For example: When youth look beyond pretty pictures, catchy captions, bling, and rented houses, they limit a lot of "fluff." Fluff is people and things that look and sound good, but in looking beyond adds no value or substance to their futures or goals.

They must recognize even the social media influencer who post half-naked pictures, pretty fingernails, money, and twerk videos is operating on a system. It's a system with the objective to connect sex, money, and beauty to worth; to systematically build likes and follows in order to sell products. By the attaching of materialism to worth, many teens are influenced in negative ways and their value systems can become skewed. This is why today's youth must fast forward in their maturation so they may "beat the systems," so to speak.

They are to steward over their energy, time, and focus on protecting their mentalities because it affects their productivity. Be discriminative and active in identifying potential threats to their minds, identities, and inner wholeness. Most importantly, having the ability and maturity to cut off access to these things when necessary. Youth should make it a ritual to be protective of their **spiritual ecosystems**.

The world should have to raise their standards because of youth displaying their intelligence. A higher intelligence that operates dimensionally with purpose and vision. **Higher intelligence** is when youth use their eyesight, insight, and knowledge to understand the things that will affect their futures. Looking ahead and seeing beyond must always be on the culture's radar. As artificial intelligence and robotics will create new things, it is up to young generations to define and establish limitations on society that will affect their sustainability.

The minds of the young generations must be anchored by the insight to solve problems before they happen. They cannot merely trust that all innovation is good. They must consider how change may affect their futures. Right now, youth should be questioning the current rise of mental illness amongst their generation and perhaps do their own research as to why.

Youth must hold themselves accountable to be a collective voice within culture and use their power of influence to respectfully protect themselves as they are valuable components of the world. Building their capacities so their minds operate at an intelligence higher than any robot of tomorrow will ever do.

This is why youth must arise beyond the distractions of popular culture and become active and productive in setting the tone, standards, codes, conducts, and ethics as a precedence for future generations to come.

Staying connected to the spiritual ecosystem is birthright protection for human identity, connectivity, the earth, and mental sustainability. What protects humanity more than any law or weapon could ever do, is the moral and ethical standards we set first for ourselves and second, those who are in positions of power and influence.

So... What's Next?

TURNING THE LIGHTS ON

To Get Woke insinuates that one must be sleeping or unaware of something that they should be educated on. The urgency for people of all ages to become more grounded in reality is evident as the entire world seems to need a wakeup call. All of creation has been signaling humanity to pay attention and Get Woke! A message spoken by the earth evident from the unusual amounts of natural disasters earthquakes, forest fires, and hurricanes.

Getting woke is just as much about seeing clearly as it is waking up. It focused a great deal on sight and its deep connection to humanity's inner and outer lives. Simply turning the lights on and looking around to what's happening is a start. Also, take inventory of everything we've covered and ask yourself hard accountability questions. How can they contribute to youth culture by sharing their knowledge and talents they have? This is a great start.

As we learned that words shape our environments, the next step youth should take is to activate themselves. Taking a move of action that will begin in the mind, heart, and soul by declaring for the future. All it takes is starting by coming with intention in purpose. Join the I Am A Vessel Youth Movement Decree of building youth culture from the inside out!

I Am A Vessel
Youth Movement Decree

I decree that every day is a new day in which I give myself permission to become stronger. I will take my rightful place of dominion and channel my focus on the things meant for my future—like my mindset, decisions, commitment, and high standards.

I decree, I will eliminate limited mindsets and behaviors, honor my time, consistently set new goals for myself, and step into my greatness day by day.

I decree and declare, I will operate in high intelligence and use my abilities and resources to elevate myself, family, and community.

I Am A Vessel, and I will use the power of my words, thoughts, and actions to fulfill my destined position to do great things for the future of myself, my family ,and my community.

Therefore, all humanity is stronger because I Am in it.

9
BRINGING IT ALL TOGETHER

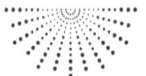

LET'S REFERENCE BACK. I AM A VESSEL WAS BIRTHED WHEN one student asked founder Sina Marie," How do you know who you are?" What the student wasn't aware of is that Sina Marie was being challenged to redefine, rediscover, and rebuild herself! That very conversation was a part of the process that built the platform.

Closing a successful business, ending a 15-year career, and risking it all to become a Vessel, which is the truest form of herself, took 3 major things mentioned in this book--- faith, revelation, and strategy! Why are these things needed? Because to build your **true** self starts with them. Our symbol is a structure for a reason. Everything in life comes with design and function.

From the piece of furniture needed to assemble to the valves inside your heart. This is the scientific correlation of who we are physically, but our spiritual structure on the inside of us has a design and function as well!

Youth must see themselves as structural design, just like the I Am A Vessel Pyramid. They and no one else will make sure they are "built" correctly.

Well, this has been a journey, and we hope this introduction to our platform has been revelatory. We hope that by reading Get Woke that you've gained a new level of awareness about who you are. We hope that youths' perspectives have shifted to inspire them beyond any challenge, situation, or circumstance they may face.

That they've seen themselves through empowering lenses of accountability. Hopefully, they've become more curious to dig deeper, broaden their perspectives, ask questions, listen wisely, and activate their inner strength, spiritual insights, and desires to live consciously and aware.

This mandate of maturity and dominion is important so that no matter how the world uproots and changes…youth have the knowledge, wisdom, and strategy to remain grounded and be the Vessels they were created to be.

Activate your power within!

Vessel Glossary©
I Am a Vessel Words, Terms & Mental Tools

VESSEL GLOSSARY

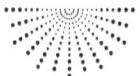

- **Belief Systems:** Standards by which we govern ourselves, make decisions and live by.

- **Balance Beam Theory:** Strategy of the balance beam used to mature emotional responses.

- **Building ourselves from the inside out™:** I Am A Vessels slogan, which is the process of self-cultivating oneself by becoming aware and knowledgeable of one's true self without any outside influences.

- **D Perspectives:** Perspectives that empower youth with mindsets to build new outcomes from certain negative behavior's.

- **Maturity Channels:** The two emotional aspects of

humanity that contain either a carnal or spiritual quality.

- **Mental Protectors:** Standards set to protect the mind.

- **Mind Innovation:** The ability for one to channel one's intelligence, perception, and intuition to function more effectively with one's thinking, reasoning, or decision making.

- **Operating by Design:** When we use our minds to capture the unseen things and used them to produce the tangible, we are operating by design.

- **Self-Unity:** I Am A Vessel term that means to agree in spirit, mind, and body. A reflection of the Divine nature of the vessel and its shape.

- **Spiritual Ecosystem:** I Am A Vessels term meaning the super genius components of human composition designed for communication with ourselves, each other, and God in connection with the Holy Spirit.

- **Technology of Vision:** Humanities ability to see with the eyes, ears, heart, soul, and intuition.

- **The 5 Vessel Lenses:** I Am A Vessels theory of lenses in which humanity views the world and life.

They are perspective, imagination, beauty, knowledge, and culture.

- **True Power:** Power that comes from within or inner power. (It is a term inspired by the process of electrical energy and how it is generated.)

- **Vessel:** A person containing special gifts inside of them for a great purpose.

- **Vessels of the Future™:** Youth generation who control their culture with positive impact and influence. It is the term in which I Am A Vessel refers to its members or potential ones.

GET WOKE WORKBOOK

Account for the journey for getting woke! Complete the assignment when you purchase your Get Woke Workbook and complete it. Available NOW!

Empowering you to BUILD & SHAPE your future.

I Am A Vessel is a creative educational platform creatively BUILDING. Creativity is the essence of everything. We are creative builders!

We are helping individuals, families, and communities: RE-DISCOVERING, RE-DEFINING, and RE-ESTABLISHING: A mandate that takes insight and vision. We teach individuals how to operate by design by developing their innate abilities. We teach them how to see, think, and build themselves creatively. Individuals learn the blueprint for being vessels. I Am A Vessel provides individuals, families, and communities with the tools and strategy to become its highest vision.

Visit our website and become a member of our community! www.iamavessel.org

Get Woke

is a tool for life

Join the I Am A Vessel Youth Movement to be the first to learn and experience our innovative learning tools and strategies such as Crea8tion Tool!

To learn more about our teachings, workshops, innovative tools contact us at youthmove@iamavessel.org

www.ingramcontent.com/pod-product-compliance
Lightning Source LLC
Chambersburg PA
CBHW030910080526
44589CB00010B/240